Content

oooooo
Preface

The main subject of this book and previous books is about results of the May 9, 2022 national elections in the Philippines.

A team of IT experts composed of the three(3) authors of these books have initiated moves to write about their findings and technical analyses of the election results.

The findings are well explained in many writings and postings in social media, particularly facebook, and the actions taken by them with the support of many sectors of society.

The updates had been recorded in previous books, published at amazondotcom, which are the following titles:

1-- Truth Petition to Comelec (Initial book)
2—Truth Warriors-1
3—Initial Stages of Truth Petition
4—Truth Warriors-2
5—Truth Patriots-1
6—Writ of Mandamus Petition
7—TNTrio Movement Book-1
8—TNTrio Movement Book-2
9—TNTrio Movement Book-3
10- TNTRIO Movement Book-4
11--TNTRIO Movement Book-5 (this one)

As this is a continuing movement, more books will be published from collection of writings and postings in the web to record all developments for posterity and guidance of all concerned.

oooooo

1
Solicitor General – Moot and Academic – Franklin Ysaac – April 23, 2023

Sharing with you the response of Solicitor General who is representing the Comelec, one of the respondents of our mandamus case .

It took their lawyer several months to file their comment which the SC issued to respondents to comment on the mandamus case which initially is a call for preservation of election data for the first hour after closing of poll.

From the periphery, as a non lawyer, they are asking the mandamus be dismissed on the basis the case is moot.

This is a favorite term by many legal and non legal people to call a case " moot and academic". Just Google this phrase and as Google says" it is a favorite phrase by law students. It describes a situation where a pending case in court loses its justiciability by virtue of supervening events so that a declaration thereon would be of no practical use or value"

This "mootness " response was used as defense by Comelec as it has already published the transmission log in their website and preservation of election data is no longer necessary because it has become moot when the transmission data was released to the public.

From a non lawyer like me and my two petitioners, it would seem the comment to dismiss the case would be sufficient for the SC to adopt their comment to dismiss the case.

This response is like saying " we are not only preserving election data, we are even releasing election data to the public" as this is mandated by law.

For them, it's game over.

But let's dissect the response closely and since they mentioned about supervening events, there are many questions that non lawyers like us can question this common evasive response.

The SG mentioned about supervening events and let us share with you supervening events before we filed the mandamus on November 3, 2022.

In July 2022 we sent letters to Comelec requesting for this simple transmission log data. In their response, they told us to go to CAC and JCOCAE. We sent letters to these two bodies but we received no response. One of our followers sent the same request and the Comelec response was they cannot release data because of " secrecy " law .

Then, last October 2022, during the forum conducted by Ateneo, Comelec disclosed the VCM results and election data that show the peak of transmission. We questioned this data as it showed the peak during the first hour could not show that there was 20M votes counted . It could only show around 10M plus votes. This revelation gave us the basis to file mandamus case before the SC as we want preservation of data.

The SC issued order to respondents to comment on our mandamus case in February 2023 but the decision was made as early as January 2023.

The respondents were given only 10 days to file comment but it took them months to respond as SG filed for extension for 30 days .

On April 3, finally the SG filed their answer which we received only a few days ago.

We are meeting with our lawyers to make the necessary response to this Comelec comment but we will wait for SC to give us their position regarding this matter.

Obviously, the SG is not fully aware or conveniently ignored the ANTECEDENTS of the case. The 100 page petition narrated in detail what transpired before we filed the mandamus case.

Speaking of antecedents including this "moot issue", they would have not released the data to the public until

Col Odoño threatened to file impeachment case against comelec officials for not releasing transmission logs.

When Comelec decided to publish in their website the alleged transmission log, we examined the transmission log and this is what we uncovered through the painstaking efforts of Eli Rio, one of petitioners :

" what was released was not the actual transmission logs because we know what transmission logs looks like . What they published was reception logs. There's a big difference between reception logs and transmission logs ".

Obviously, Comelec was not careful in disclosing which data to release .

Worse, the reception logs contain information that do not match the ER or election returns time logs.

Please take note that ERs are produced by VCM and each political party including Ppcrv gets a copy.

In the investigation done by Eli Rio, he discovered the time log differentials between the time and date ERs were printed and distributed and the time log these were transmitted via telco to the transparency server.

What is unconscionable is that the ERs were released and time stamped much later than the Transmission log time stamped minutes, and even hours before ERs were printed and released to political parties.

What do you call this disparity then between time stamp of ER and TL?

This cannot be considered or called " moot". SG will have his hands full explaining this act of deception by Comelec.

All these differentials were disclosed by Eli Rio in his posts.

On the basis of this revelation by Eli, he signed a judicial affidavit and our lawyer filed a week ago a supplemental petition to the mandamus case requesting Comelec to explain the discrepancies between the October peak data and published data and now the ER versus the publisher Transmission Logs which make the case more glaring in terms of manipulation or data rigging by Comelec.

The SG has a lot more explaining to do when it receives a copy of our supplemental petition.

But the case doesn't end there. This ER vs Transmission Log data differential is a huge potential case which we will look into when we meet again with our lawyer.

This circus of playing with election data puts comelec in dire straits and while they are playing with this data, we collect them and study them before we make our next case before the SC or another court.

We shall keep you posted on new developments about this case after we meet with our lawyer.

Today, our prayer group will meet before the Comelec office in Intramuros at 9 am to offer prayers to these officials like what our prayer group did during the vigil before the SC last November which lasted 3 months until SC issued the order to respondents to give their comments.

The SG gave their comment already and the explanation that this is "moot" because of antecedents will be challenged based on our own description of antecedents including the flipflopping on which data they want to release.

We shall continue to play on court or off court about the election fiasco until the truth finally comes out .

The following SG response is shared with you so you can file and make your comments too.

Republic of the Philippines
SUPREME COURT
Manila

<u>En Banc</u>

ELISEO MIJARES RIO, JR., AUGUSTO CADELIÑA LAGMAN, and FRANKLIN FAYLOGA YSAAC,

Petitioners,

- versus -   **GR. No. 263838**

COMMISSION ON ELECTIONS (COMELEC), SMARTMATIC TOTAL INFORMATION MANAGEMENT, DITO TELECOMMUNITY, GLOBE TELECOM, and SMART COMMUNICATIONS,

Respondents.

x-------------------------------------x

COMMENT

Respondent **COMMISSION ON ELECTIONS (COMELEC)**, through the **OFFICE OF THE SOLICITOR GENERAL (OSG)**, in compliance with this Honorable Court's 10 January 10 Resolution, a copy of which was received by the COMELEC on 21 February 2023, respectfully submits this Comment and states:

PREFATORY STATEMENT

1.   As taxpayers, petitioners Eliseo Mijares Rio, Jr., Augusto Cadelina Lagman, and Franklin Fayloga Ysaac filed the instant Petition for *Mandamus* with the following prayer:

WHEREFORE, PREMISES CONSIDERED, it is most respectfully prayed of the Honorable Supreme Court:

COMMENT
Rio, Jr., et al. v. COMELEC, et al.
G.R. No. 263838
x--x

1.   A Temporary Restraining Order (TRO) be issued immediately enjoining the respondents to cease and desist from any act that may modify/erase/delete any part or whole of the historically important subscriber/cyber traffic data log integrity/call record details corresponding to national election results transmitted from 7PM to at least 9PM of 09 May 2022;

2.   After due hearing before 09 November 2022, and/or on the basis of judicial notice of history, an ancillary writ of preliminary mandatory injunction be issued, directing the private respondent telecommunication companies (telcos) to deliver faithful copies of their respective records/details of the said historically-important data directly and exclusively to the Honorable Supreme Court; and

3.   After due hearing, a final writ of mandamus be issued directing the respondents to preserve for posterity the said historically-important data.

Other reliefs just and equitable are also prayed for.[1]

ANTECEDENTS

2.   On 9, May 2022, the national and local elections were held in the entire country through the automated election system using Vote-Counting Machines (VCMs). Petitioners claim that they observed certain irregularities during said elections. They specifically cite the high volume of transmissions on the first hour after the closing of the elections. Hence, they wrote respondents several letters from 22 July 2022 to October 2022[2] essentially requesting them to explain the supposed anomalies. In a letter dated 15 August 2022,[3] the COMELEC referred petitioners to the COMELEC Advisory Council (CAC) and the Joint Congressional Oversight Committee on Automated Election System (JCOC-AES), explaining that they are the proper bodies having custody of the documents they were requesting.

3.   Without awaiting the response of the other respondents, petitioners then filed the present Petition for

---

[1] Petition, p. 19.
[2] Id., p. 3, par. 9; p. 11, par. 15.
[3] Annex "H" of the Petition.

COMMENT
Rio, Jr., et al. v. COMELEC, et al.
G.R. No. 263838
x------------------------------------x

1.   A Temporary Restraining Order (TRO) be issued immediately enjoining the respondents to cease and desist from any act that may modify/erase/delete any part or whole of the historically important subscriber/cyber traffic data log integrity/call record details corresponding to national election results transmitted from 7PM to at least 9PM of 09 May 2022;

2.   After due hearing before 09 November 2022, and/or on the basis of judicial notice of history, an ancillary writ of preliminary mandatory injunction be issued, directing the private respondent telecommunication companies (telcos) to deliver faithful copies of their respective records/details of the said historically-important data directly and exclusively to the Honorable Supreme Court; and

3.   After due hearing, a final writ of mandamus be issued directing the respondents to preserve for posterity the said historically-important data.

Other reliefs just and equitable are also prayed for.

2.   Notably, the petitioners' purpose for filing the Petition for *Mandamus* is to compel respondents "to preserve the subscriber/cyber traffic data log integrity/call record details corresponding to national election results transmitted from 7PM to at least 9PM of 09 May 2022"[5] or, in short, the transmission logs of the 9 May 2022 elections. Petitioners accused the COMELEC of hiding such "historical data."[6] They assert that that the Petition "does not violate the Data Privacy Act because this Petition is just praying for **data preservation = not for releasing sensitive data to the petitioners.**"[7]

3.   It bears stressing that the COMELEC had previously submitted the logs to the Joint Congressional Oversight Committee (JCOC), the lawful custodian thereof, as early as the third quarter of 2022 in full compliance with Republic Act (R.A.) No. 8436, as amended by R.A. No. 9369. At any rate, the COMELEC did more than what petitioners ask from this Honorable Court.

---

[5] Id., p. 19.
[6] Id., p. 2.
[7] Id., p. 3, par. 9; emphasis supplied.

4

4.   On 22 March 2023, the COMELEC released and uploaded in its official website the List of VCM Transmission Logs of the 9 May 2022 national and local elections. The COMELEC uploaded not only the files containing the "List of VCM Received During First Hour of Transmission May 9, 2022 NLE" which petitioners seek to be preserved, but also the "List of VCM Received Entire Transmission Logs May 9, 2022 NLE."[8] The decision to make the data publicly available was to erase doubts on the credibility of the automated election system. With the publication of the transmission logs, the public can access more information regarding the election process, essential to guaranteeing accountability and transparency in the country's electoral system.

5.   Plainly, the present Petition for *Mandamus* is dismissible on the ground of mootness. A case becomes "moot" when it ceases to present a justiciable controversy by supervening events so that a declaration thereon would be of no practical use or value. Here, the publication of the transmission logs of the 9 May 2022 national and local Elections has rendered the Petition moot and academic.

6.   A case becomes moot when there is no more actual controversy between the parties or no useful purpose can be served in passing upon the merits. Courts will not determine a moot question in a case in which no practical relief can be granted. It is unnecessary to indulge in academic discussion of a case presenting a moot question, as a judgment thereon cannot have any practical legal effect or, in the nature of things, cannot be enforced.[9]

7.   In *Garcia v. COMELEC*,[10] this Honorable Court held that where the issues have become moot and academic, there is no justiciable controversy, thereby rendering the resolution of the same of no practical use or value.

8.   Similarly, in *Gancho-on v. Secretary of Labor and Employment*,[11] this Honorable Court ruled that:

---

[8] https://comelec.gov.ph/?r=2022NLE/VCM_2022NLE_TRANSMISSION_LOGS last accessed on March 24, 2023; copies of the Certifications from the COMELEC are likewise attached as Annexes "A" and "B".
[9] *Baldo v. COMELEC, et al.*, G.R. No. 176135, June 16, 2009.
[10] 328 Phil. 288 (1996).
[11] 337 Phil. 654, 658 (1997).

COMMENT
Rio, Jr., et al. v. COMELEC, et al.
G.R. No. 263838
x--x

It is a rule of universal application, almost, that courts of justice constituted to pass upon substantial rights will not consider questions in which no actual interests are involved; they decline jurisdiction of moot cases. And where the issue has become moot and academic, there is no justiciable controversy, so that a declaration thereon would be of no practical use or value. There is no actual substantial relief to which petitioners would be entitled and which would be negated by the dismissal of the petition.

PRAYER

WHEREFORE, it is respectfully prayed that the instant Petition for *Mandamus* be **DISMISSED** on the ground of mootness.

Other forms of relief, just and equitable under the premises, are likewise prayed for.

Makati City for Manila, April 3, 2023.

MENARDO I. GUEVARRA
Solicitor General
Roll No. 33957
IBP No. 292878; January 9, 2023; Bulacan
MCLE Exemption No. VII-EXD000076; August 13, 2019

B. MARC A. CANUTO
Assistant Solicitor General
(On Leave)
Roll No. 42237
IBP Lifetime Member No. 09130; April 28, 2010
MCLE Exemption No. VIII-OSG000043; April 21, 2022

COMMENT
Rio, Jr., et al. v. COMELEC, et al.
G.R. No. 263838
x--------------------------------x

NOEL CEZAR T. SEGOVIA
Senior State Solicitor
(Officer-in-Charge)
Roll No. 40524
IBP No. 199487 ; January 3, 2023
MCLE Compliance No. VII-0021137; June 23, 2022

PAOLO V. QUETULIO
Senior State Solicitor
Roll No. 50362
IBP Lifetime Member No. 05658; January 30, 2006
MCLE Compliance No. VII-0018128; May 17, 2022

OFFICE OF THE SOLICITOR GENERAL
134 Amorsolo Street, Legaspi Village, Makati City
Tel. No. 8988-1674
Email: efile@osg.gov.ph

Copy furnished:

Atty. Kates Jastin E. Aguilar
c/o Eliseo Rio, Jr.
Lot 7, Block 11, Soldiers Hill
Barangay Putatan
1772 Muntinlupa City
katesjastin@gmail.com
eliseoriojr27@gmail.com
guslagman2019@gmail.com
ffysaac@gmail.com

BMC/PVQ/len: 23-004756

oooooo

2
DIRECT EVIDENCE THAT THE 2022 ELECTION WAS RIGGED – Eliseo Rio Jr.

This proof of fraudulent data came from the"List of VCM Received May 9, 2022 NLE" that COMELEC itself uploaded in its website. How could three clustered precincts have exactly the same number of actual voters who voted at an unbelievable 1,000 people, immediately followed by a precinct with 0 voter? How could an official document of COMELEC contain so many anomalies (we have shown and will show more irregularities where ERs of precincts were received by the Transparency Server even HOURS BEFORE these ERs were transmitted by the VCMs) still be considered the result of a clean and honest election?

LIST OF VCM RECEIVED MAY 9, 2022 NLE

NO.	CLUSTERED	ACTUAL	RECEPTION DATETIME
105951	39141532	593	11-May-2022 15:54:40
105952	39141533	416	11-May-2022 15:56:44
105953	39141504	482	11-May-2022 15:58:43
105954	36070018	439	11-May-2022 15:59:52
105955	39101368	278	11-May-2022 16:01:25
105956	92120282	0	11-May-2022 16:02:27
105957	39141511	453	11-May-2022 16:03:15
105958	36070006	655	11-May-2022 16:18:21
105959	36070014	3	11-May-2022 16:32:21
105960	92120253	1,000	11-May-2022 17:19:39
105961	92120230	1,000	11-May-2022 17:21:34
105962	92120232	1,000	11-May-2022 17:23:09
105963	92120275	0	11-May-2022 17:24:27
105964	66120038	3	11-May-2022 17:44:51
105965	36120032	324	11-May-2022 17:58:26
105966	38100034	528	11-May-2022 18:01:45
105967	38280033	445	11-May-2022 18:09:22
105968	07010125	434	11-May-2022 18:17:12

Oooooo

No.

Ronnie Adriano Amoroso
FYI - this is the E-mail Reply from the TELCO SMART dated April 24, 2023

Franklin Ysaac
Ronnie Adriano Amoroso Ronnie thank you for sharing but this is not their reply to our mandamus case

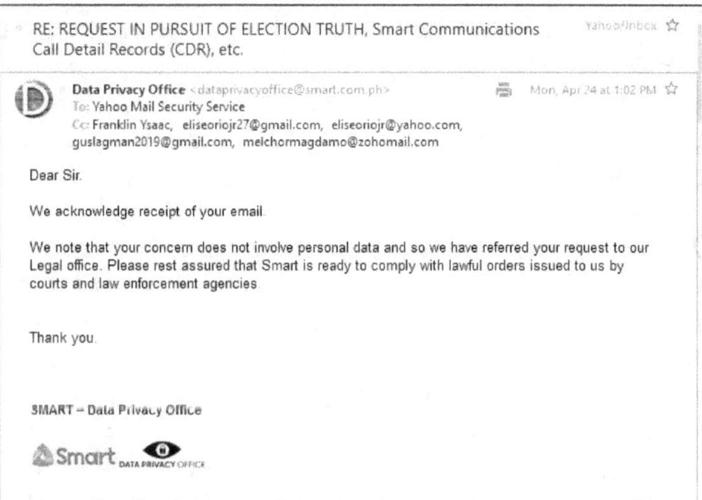

RE: REQUEST IN PURSUIT OF ELECTION TRUTH, Smart Communications Call Detail Records (CDR), etc.   Yahoo/Inbox ☆

Data Privacy Office <dataprivacyoffice@smart.com.ph>   Mon, Apr 24 at 1:02 PM ☆
To: Yahoo Mail Security Service
Cc: Franklin Ysaac, eliseoriojr27@gmail.com, eliseoriojr@yahoo.com, guslagman2019@gmail.com, melchormagdamo@zohomail.com

Dear Sir.

We acknowledge receipt of your email.

We note that your concern does not involve personal data and so we have referred your request to our Legal office. Please rest assured that Smart is ready to comply with lawful orders issued to us by courts and law enforcement agencies.

Thank you.

SMART – Data Privacy Office

OOOOOO

3
My 2016 Article -
Franklin Ysaac – April 2023

I wrote this piece 7 years ago during the 2016 Philippine elections.

Sad that the Presidency was snatched by a candidate who proved to be the one of the most disastrous Presidents next to the dictator.

I was probably dreaming of a Utopian political system where real democracy which was a gift from the Greek political system but which just remains a pipe dream to this day.

I didn't dream to be one of the proponents and advocates of a true democracy as I happened to be one of the trio who questioned the results of the 2022 election.

We are now almost one year from commemorating death of our democracy but we will prevail as TNTrio will exhaust all its efforts and energies to bring back real and true democracy to the people.

It's not game over for us. It's game over for them.

May God press the button to allow us to finish the job of wrapping up the truth and letting truth take over our elections.

Franklin Ysaac Article

Now that Philippine elections is on its homestretch, we wonder who the next leader will be and whether he or she will prove to be worthy of the position he or she will be holding for the next six years. Looking back at history of Philippine Presidents, I have only known one who was worthy of such position and sad to say he left the Presidency with much unfinished business. He was a President who truly deserved to be the nation's leader and who was loved by all Filipinos until fate stole him from us on that fateful and tragic day in March 1957. I was only seven years old then not knowing much about Philippine politics. His death left a big void in Presidencies who followed after him. None of these Presidents has been very much admired and until today, much remains to be desired and expected from the candidates. As a student of the Philippine political system which almost copied the American Presidential system, we will never be able to achieve the kind of Presidency we had earlier after the Americans gave us back our independence. Political patronage rather than issues or concerns continue to dominate the political landscape every election time. A time for a big change in this 2016 elections? This will not happen. A new political system and order in the same way that reforms are being introduced in the Philippine Congress should be introduced. We tested the parliamentary system already and we failed. One candidate is introducing federal system and this will not work. The local government system is already in place but controls should be introduced as many local leaders have been passing laws that go against national interest. I am an advocate of a strong local leadership with less dependence on the national leadership except for funding for health, education which many local governments are unable to support. A common ground will be strong economic performance of each local government where business and employment are encouraged. Peace and order shall remain in the hands of national leadership. Overall, each local government must not enact laws that will go against the national interest in terms of sacrificing our environment, sovereignty, defense, health and education of the general public. And where does the office of the Presidency take its power or the senate? Electing the President or senators on a national scale is a very expensive process. Each local government will elects its own senators and congressmen and who in turn will elect the President and giving the President to choose his cabinet who will still be vetted by Congress. Such President who fails to perform may be recalled similar to a parliamentary system where a new President may be elected by the same Congress. We have not tested this yet. If you read the political systems introduced by the Romans and the Greeks surely we will learn from their discourses on the best political system. Too bad there are no more Roman and Greek survivors but the philosopher kings from Plato to Aristotle have been replaced by political patronage which continues to this day where money influences the course or destiny of nations. So, my fellow Filipinos, much as i want change to happen in our beloved country I do not see this coming in the next six years nor in the subsequent Philippine elections unless we address the kind of political system we truly deserve. I miss President Ramon Magsaysay who i still consider to be the best servant leader of our country.

oooooo

4

COMELEC, STOP THE DECEPTIONS! - by TNTRIO Movement – May 2023

Deception #1. The Transparency Server (TS) started receiving VCM transmitted Election Returns (ER) at 7:08 pm of May 9, 2022. THIS IS IMPOSSIBLE! It is illegal for any precinct to close BEFORE the official time of 7pm as this might disenfranchise a voter who arrives just before 7pm. The COMELEC General Instructions require that 9 major tasks must first be performed by the teacher members of the Electoral Board (ER) BEFORE the VCM can transmit its ER to the TS. Of the 9 tasks, printing 8 copies of both the National and Local ERs already takes 12 minutes to accomplish. The other tasks would take another 7 minutes as timed in an Instruction Demo Video made by COMELEC itself. Therefore, the earliest time that VCMs could transmit their ERs would be 7:19pm, NOT 7:08pm.

Deception #2. The Transparency Server was able to count 20M+ votes which was shown to the public on 8:02pm of May 9, 2022. Again, THIS IS IMPOSSIBLE. We are not questioning the transmission speed of the ERs, nor the number of bits of data these contain, as COMELEC is just muddling the issue. What we ARE saying is that the 20M+ votes cannot be received and counted by the TS by 8:02pm because VCM transmissions started at 7:19pm and NOT at the deceptive time of 7:08pm.

Deception #3. The data uploaded in the COMELEC website were Transmission Logs as announced by COMELEC Chairman George Garcia himself. THIS IS A BLATANT LIE. What was uploaded and shown to the public were Reception Logs. Transmission Logs are data that come from VCM transmissions while Reception Logs are received data coming from the Transparency Server. In a CLEAN AND HONEST ELECTION, the Transmission Logs MUST JIBE with the Reception Logs. But on October 18, 2022, COMELEC showed the public Accumulated VCM Transmissions that PEAKED at the SECOND HOUR after transmissions started. This DID NOT JIBED with the Transparency Server receptions that PEAKED at the FIRST HOUR after voting closed. The Transmission Logs we were asking for were the basis used by COMELEC IT personnel to plot the graph "Accumulated VCM Transmissions" shown on October 18. Instead what was deceptively shown to us were Reception Logs of the TS.

Deception #4. COMELEC says that whatever irregularities observed BEFORE the 2022 Election no longer matter because watchdogs like PPCRV, NAMFREL and LENTI have observed very high accuracy in the election results. These irregularities included the possible change in the program downloaded in all VCMs observed by NAMFREL, the configuring of SD cards and printing of ballots WITHOUT any witnesses as required by law, the sudden change in the protocol on how Smartmatic transmits the data from 3G to 4G which could prevent auditors from tracing from which VCM the ER was transmitted, the choice of the logistic company, hacking of Smartmatic data, etc. THIS IS THE WORST DECEPTION. These irregularities can in fact lead to deceiving the watchdogs and the public into believing that there was nothing irregular in the election because the results were accurate. Just like in a clever magic trick, the seemingly impossible happens because of deceptions and illusions that were carefully prepared before the performance.

STOP THE DECEPTIONS. JUST SHOW THE REAL TRANSMISSION LOGS CORROBORATED BY THE CDR OF TELCOS.

oooooo

5
Eliseo Rio Jr – posted this link – copy and paste in your browser

https://l.facebook.com/l.php?u=https%3A%2F%2Fwww.
change.org%2Fp%2Fpeople-s-mandamus-to-compel-
comelec-to-disclose-true-transmission-
logs%3Frecruiter%3D1228008033%26utm_source%3Ds
hare_petition%26utm_medium%3Dfacebook%26utm_ca
mpaign%3Dpsf_combo_share_initial%26utm_term%3Dp
sf_combo_share_initial%26recruited_by_id%3D5ed91a8
0-2141-11ec-9032-
33ae8712f406%26share_bandit_exp%3Dinitial-
35876111-en-US%26utm_content%3Dfht-35876111-en-
us%253A0%26mibextid%3DZxz2cZ%26fbclid%3DIwAR
1pTkta0-_KGgbApnxeqVjqoJZh-
jFjwTExH1E1QqXP4lW_PHMJAvjuoOU&h=AT1RVqFLZ
H82QqwJPA3iUnaiEnBeq1in3gvwYfsYLw7XG3sRNwqf
BPQJqSqd46uzaX5xeQZE_KSSGX8392HihL1Sr26HpH
hqiaVuwL54nogeWt_ieDDYFmfRPDCmjNmhJ6e-
&__tn__=R]-
R&c[0]=AT2ASLaZjouxgw2S4kAJgMp_iZsLF7O7sP6W
RoglZyFzyu0nvoXjfK7WnYw51Qaf19W0p4AqKFP0yJ3K
O6hPstXbk5ANTGEeQ2qC94j_Q7wnAgBy1YPVqzNm6
O6nfXL9zwKxXR57yQpwFmJQmQgYFq6sv_D2hZEFIL
vbLMGR2N4OwdzFss4

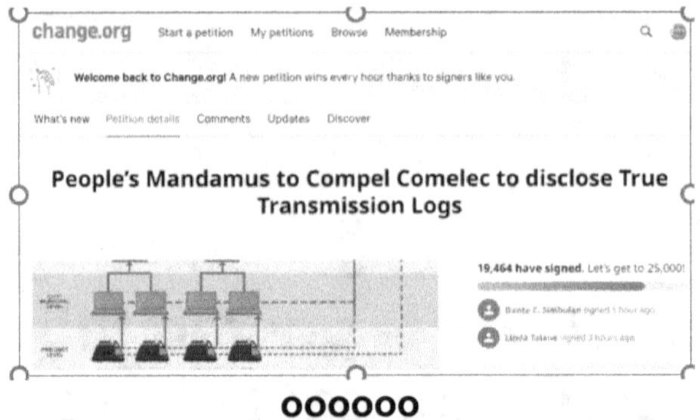

oooooo

6
One year of TNTRIO Movement for Truth - Franklin Ysaac – April 28, 2023

Sa simula, ang TNTrio ay mag isa sa kampanya sa katotohanan at isa isa namulat ang milyong taga subaybay at nagkaroon ng pag asa ang mga nadismaya sa resulta ng eleksyon!

Mag isang taon na ang kampanya sa Mayo at ang pag asa ay nagbunga na at sa awa ng Panginoon ay magtatagumpay ang kampanya ng taumbayan at ang katotohanan ang magwawagi at ang mga may sala ay tatanggap ng kanilang parusa !

Maraming Salamat Panginoon !

Amen .

(Translation in English)

In the beginning, the TNTrio campaigned alone in the truth and one by one million of followers woke up and those who were disappointed with the election results got hope!

It's been a year since the May campaign and the hope has come to fruition and by the grace of God the people's campaign will succeed and the truth will prevail and the guilty will receive their punishment !

Thank you so much Lord !
Amen

oooooo

7
PUBLIC DEBATE - ARAW NG DAYAAN SA COMELEC

Paranaque City
March 24, 2023
Atty. George Erwin M. Garcia
Chairman, Commission on Elections
Intramuros, Manila
SUBJECT: PUBLIC DEBATE - ARAW NG DAYAAN SA COMELEC
Dear Mr. Chairman,
It has occurred to me that May 9,2023 is first anniversary ng **Araw ng Dayaan sa Comelec**.

You might want to make it a holy day for your organization, Sir, by you coming clean on the questions and issues I raised to you in my March 29, 2023, **in a public debate** between General Rio and myself on one side, and you, Sir, and the six other Commissioners on the other side. You might want to bring with you, Sir, your bloggers, supposedly from Namfrel, as your resource persons – they who continue to claim, falsely, that there were no irregularities in the last election – when Namfrel, in an official report to Comelec, itself disclosed it found software flaws in the election system, and **warned Comelec of possible cheating.**

I hope, Sir, after 59 days of hesitation and self-examination since my March 29, 2023 letter to you, you may be able to honestly answer my questions, during our debate:

1.   Why did you release to me and General Rio Reception Logs – Deception Logs if I may call it correctly – instead of the proof of transmission of the 20m votes, the Transmission Logs from precinct level to the Transparency Server of Comelec, which releases partial and unofficial results. Didn't you deceive me and General Rio, and the public, Sir, into believing you were finally releasing the Transmission Logs, to us. If you did, and I believe you did, bakit po, Sir? Dahil po ba wala naman talaga yung 20million votes? Ask ko lang po kung saan kaya nanggaling yun?

2.   Your official Comelec accumulated VCM reports graph presented by Comelec itself in a public forum on election sponsored by Ateneo University on October 18, 2023, shows the accumulated votes peaking at 12 million votes in an hour after close of election on May 9, 2023. However, the Deception Logs, released to me and General Rio, on March 23, 2023, showed accumulated votes peaking at 20m+ votes. Same Comelec reports on accumulated votes in the same one-hour period showing different accumulated votes peaking at 12m votes and 20m votes, respectively?

3.   Saan po ninyo kinuha yung nadagdag na 8m votes? Hindi po kaya pre-loaded yung votes na reported as unofficial, partial reports from the unofficial server of Comelec? Could these things have happened as "the result of software flaws" as revealed by Namfrel, or mere "typo errors" Comelec want us to believe? And why did Comelec ignore Namfrel's warning of possible cheating?

4.   What took Comelec all of 252 days, from when the TNT Trio first asked for the proof of transmission of the 20m votes, to respond to us? Ganun na po ba kahirap at katagal mag-doctor ng transmission reports? Didn't you violate our constitutional right when

you deliberately ignored the 15-day deadline required by law to respond to a request for information like ours?

5.   My final question, Sir, meron po ba talaga yung 20m votes?

Mr. Chairman, the public debate, streamed to the Filipino people live or replay, should enlighten them if their votes went to the candidates they voted for, or if SmartMagic and its co-conspirators played a cruel game on them. At the same time, the public debate shall provide you the opportunity to explain your side of each issue.

Very truly yours,
Col. Leonardo O. Odoño (Ret.)
PMA Class of 1964
A Filipino

oooooo

8
AN OPEN LETTER TO VP LENI ROBREDO – Roman Zarate – April 29, 2023

Being one of your very many supporters, please allow me to dare make an observation and suggestion to you.

1. Your silence in the wake of the Mandamus petition of the TNTrio has baffled and confused many of your supporters. They understood why you initially accepted the proclamation of Marcos and Sara. However, after your period of foreign speaking engagements and Angat Buhay projects, they now look to you for leadership and support in the efforts of the TNTrio and others to show that the election was rigged.

2. Please communicate with Gen Eliseo Rio and the TNTrio to understand what they are working hard to achieve against all odds and somehow show the people that you support their efforts to LEARN THE TRUTH. Your supporters and even the Liberal Party are now rudderless and many have lost heart for the fight for true justice and democracy in the Philippines.

Many are puzzled by your silence and have even wondered whether you are truly the leader we had all hoped for. Some have even spoken about giving up the fight and not voting in the next elections because it would be useless in the face of a biased COMELEC.

Where once hundreds of thousands and even millions rallied to your side, now not even 25 thousand have signed an online petition supporting the Mandamus petition.

Please come out once again and lead the people who are crying for justice and true democracy for our country. At this time, no other person exists who can do what ONLY YOU CAN. That is, to UNITE us once again. The country is crying out for your leadership.

PLEASE LEAD US NOW ...

Fred-Cyd Gallardo

Magpirma po tayo sa PEOPLE'S MANDAMUS:

https://chng.it/79gg9SqWmq

People's Mandamus to Compel Comelec to disclose True Transmission Logs. PLEASE SIGN AND SHARE THIS! You do not have to "CHIP IN".

oooooo

9
Franklin Ysaac explains again – April 30, 2023

Let me cut this whole matter of fraudulent results into this scenario which I described last year and which was validated by the expose of my colleague Eli Rio:

1. Smartmatic provided the automated election system which is a seamless process or straight through processing from casting of ballot, to counting , to printing of election returns and transmission reports.

2. The automated election system was witnessed by independent IT and was presumed to be perfect .

3. During the actual automated election process, the system was cut into parts which overrode the approved automated system.

4. The ERs were produced and the transmission reports were made.

5. The ERs and Transmission reports were given to political parties and ppcrv. The political parties kept the ERs but did not keep the transmission reports. These transmission reports eventually faded as the papers used were thermal paper.

6. We asked for copies of these transmission reports but we were ignored.

7. The ERs were eventually transmitted via telcos and were recorded under call detail reports.

8. We filed mandamus before SC to preserve the election data . Response was moot because they published the transmission logs.

9. We filed supplemental petition because the published transmission logs were not true and they were merely reception logs.

10. The whole process which was supposed to be seamless or straight through never happened. The ERs time logs do not reflect the same time logs even in reception logs. The ERs were transmitted much much later than the published reception logs giving rise to falsification of data.

11. The time logs from VCMs via Telco to Transparency server are supposed to be synchronized.

13. But what happened to the election data which passed through telcos but didn't end up in the transmission servers?

My judgment as IT is where is the real server or transparency server ?

In my Fb post last year, I mentioned that there is a strong possibility there are at least two transparency servers. One which is pre loaded and another which is the true transparency server ?

Questions:

A.Where are these data which were supposed to be transmitted by telco to the real server?

B. Who ordered the changes

In the automated system which is apparently not a seamless or straight through processing system ?

C. It the changes showed the apparent and perhaps deliberate attempt to change the results of the election, then those officials responsible have committed a serious crime?

We are closely studying this case and we will discuss this with our lawyers to make our case credible and irrefutable.

oooooo

10
What's going on at PPCRV - TNTrio Movement – Mhel Mendez Bulabos – April 30, 2023

What's going on with PPCRV?

Ppcrv boasts of having all the data with them— precinct-level transmissions, votes cast for whom, from which locations, etc. Yet PPCRV says they could not release the data because they signed a "non-disclosure agreement" with Comelec. Where there is a public interest contrary to Comelec policy, the role of a citizen watchdog is to side with the people rather than stay in the good graces of an opaque Comelec that treats it like its show dog.

oooooo

11
COMELEC's Chairman George Garcia desperate move to muddle the issue -
Eliseo Rio Jr – May 2023

In COMELEC's desperate move to muddle the issue, Chairman George Garcia, in a recent press conference, tried to confuse the public by saying that it is very possible to transmit 20M+ votes in the FIRST HOUR after voting closed at 7pm of May 9, 2022. He said that such number of votes is contained in just around 39,500 Election Returns (ER) sent by an equal number of VCMs. He said that an average picture sent by an ordinary cellphone contains more data than around 10 ERs. And he emphasized to the public that such a picture can be transmitted in a split second.

BUT WE ARE NOT QUESTIONING the speed of transmission of the ERs nor the digital data content of each. We have pointed out, and COMELEC has never refuted us, that the 20M+ votes shown to the public at 8:02pm of May 9, 2022, IS ONLY possible IF VCM transmissions started at 7:08pm, May 9,2022, as shown in the Reception Logs uploaded by COMELEC IN THEIR WEBSITE on March 23, 2023.

It is the STARTING TIME OF 7:08pm in the Reception Logs that we ARE QUESTIONING, NOT THE TRANSMISSION SPEED NOR THE DIGITAL CONTENT OF THE ERs! From the time and motion study required to accomplish the 9 major tasks after closing of voting to actual transmission of the ERs, the printing of 8 copies of the ER alone TOOK 12 MINUTES TO FINISH. The other 8 major tasks took another 7 MINUTES or a total of 19 MINUTES. The earliest time that VCM Transmissions could have started would be 7:19pm NOT 7:08pm. WHAT WE ARE SAYING IS THAT IF VCM TRANSMISSIONS STARTED AT 7:19PM, IT WOULD BE IMPOSSIBLE FOR THE TRANSPARENCY SERVER TO HAVE RECEIVED AND COUNTED 20M+ VOTES BY 8:02PM OF MAY 9, 2022.

HERE IS A CASE IN POINT, where a precinct in Barayong Elementary School, Palo, Leyte, obviously closed some 10 minutes before the official closing time of 7pm. It was able to print its first ER at 7:02:42pm. Yet in the Reception Log shown by COMELEC in its website, this same ER containing the actual votes of 342 voters was received by the Transparency Server (TS) at 10:26:33pm, or more than 3 hours after the ER was printed. In most precincts in the rural areas, transmitting the ERs was a problem because of poor telco signals. But the same Reception Log showed several anomalies where the TS received the ERs several minutes, even hours, BEFORE these ERS were being printed.

That is why COMELEC must show the actual Transmission Logs, verified thru the Telcos CDRs, so that it can be compared with the Reception Logs it uploaded in its website which is full of anomalous data. It must stop deceiving the people that the Reception Logs are the same as the Transmission Logs. COMELEC had actually shown the Transmission Logs in a graph "Accumulated VCM Transmissions" on October 18, 2022 which PEAKED at the SECOND HOUR after transmissions started, in stark contrast with with Transparency Server received data that PEAKED at the FIRST HOUR after voting closed.

IN A CLEAN AND HONEST ELECTION, THE VCM TRANSMISSION LOGS MUST MATCH THE RECEPTION LOGS OF THE TRANSPARENCY SERVER. IF IT DOES NOT, THEN THE 2022 ELECTION WAS RIGGED, NO MATTER HOW ACCURATE THE RESULTS OBSERVED BY SO-CALLED WATCHDOGS MAY SAY.

78890	12220011	628	09-May-2022 22:26:33
78891	16020038	635	09-May-2022 22:26:33
78892	37390025	342	09-May-2022 22:26:33
78893	56220121	610	09-May-2022 22:26:33
78894	82110021	595	09-May-2022 22:26:33
78895	05030066	726	09-May-2022 22:26:34

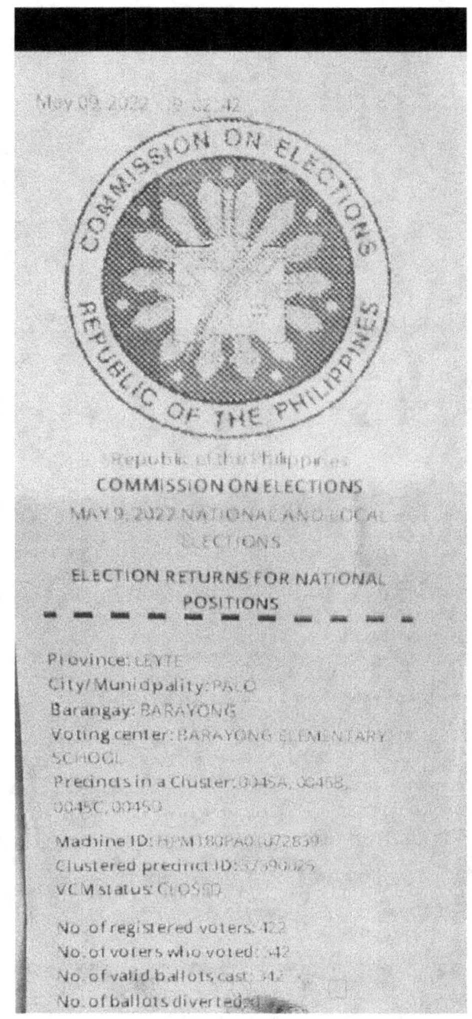
May 09, 2022 18:52:42
Republic of the Philippines
COMMISSION ON ELECTIONS
MAY 9, 2022 NATIONAL AND LOCAL
ELECTIONS
ELECTION RETURNS FOR NATIONAL
POSITIONS
Province: LEYTE
City/Municipality: PALO
Barangay: BARAYONG
Voting center: BARAYONG ELEMENTARY
SCHOOL
Precincts in a Cluster: 0045A, 0045B,
0045C, 0045D
Machine ID: H/M180PA0J072839
Clustered precinct ID: 37490025
VCM status: CLOSED
No. of registered voters: 423
No. of voters who voted: 342
No. of valid ballots cast: 342
No. of ballots diverted:

COMELEC GARCIA MANLILINLANG!
RECEPTION LOGS ANG IBINIGAY SA HALIP NA TRANSMISSION LOGS!
Why would COMELEC Chairman George Garcia tell the public that the May 9 Election Transmission Logs will be released when what were given are actually Reception Logs? It is precisely the Reception data of the Servers that is being questioned. We need the VCM Transmissions data to check whether the unbelievable 20M+ votes counted in the Transparency Server (TS) in the first hour after voting closed at 7pm of May 9, 2022, were actually transmitted by the VCMs. Of course the Reception Logs will tally with what the TS received and showed the public. But will the VCMs Tansmission Logs tally with the Servers' Reception Logs? If COMELEC is deceiving the public, that means it is hiding something.
Eliseo Rio Jr.
March 29, 2023
Fred Santos
COMMISSION ON ELECTIONS
ILABAS ANG TELCO RECORDS NOW!
HUWAG TATANTANAN
SMART GLOBE COMELEC
REPUBLIC PHILIPPINES
Fred Santos

oooooo

12
THE BASIC QUESTION – WHERE DID THE 20 MILLION VOTES COME FROM? – STILL NO VALID ANSWER FROM COMELEC, EXCEPT MUDDLING THE ISSUE REPEATEDLY. – Eliseo Rio Jr. – May 2023

TNTrio Movement
Eliseo Rio Jr · ·
https://www.facebook.com/1026127023/posts/10226288728897723/?mibextid=DcJ9fc
Eliseo Rio Jr

In COMELEC's desperate move to muddle the issue, Chairman George Garcia, in a recent press conference, tried to confuse the public by saying that it is very possible to transmit 20M+ votes in the FIRST

HOUR after voting closed at 7pm of May 9, 2022. He said that such number of votes is contained in just around 39,500 Election Returns (ER) sent by an equal number of VCMs. He said that an average picture sent by an ordinary cellphone contains more data than around 10 ERs. And he emphasized to the public that such a picture can be transmitted in a split second.

BUT WE ARE NOT QUESTIONING the speed of transmission of the ERs nor the digital data content of each. We have pointed out, and COMELEC has never refuted us, that the 20M+ votes shown to the public at 8:02pm of May 9, 2022, IS ONLY possible IF VCM transmissions started at 7:08pm, May 9,2022, as shown in the Reception Logs uploaded by COMELEC IN THEIR WEBSITE on March 23, 2023.

It is the STARTING TIME OF 7:08pm in the Reception Logs that we ARE QUESTIONING, NOT THE TRANSMISSION SPEED NOR THE DIGITAL CONTENT OF THE ERs! From the time and motion study required to accomplish the 9 major tasks after closing of voting to actual transmission of the ERs, the printing of 8 copies of the ER alone TOOK 12 MINUTES TO FINISH. The other 8 major tasks took another 7 MINUTES or a total of 19 MINUTES. The earliest time that VCM Transmissions could have started would be 7:19pm NOT 7:08pm. WHAT WE ARE SAYING IS THAT IF VCM TRANSMISSIONS STARTED AT 7:19PM, IT WOULD BE IMPOSSIBLE FOR THE TRANSPARENCY SERVER TO HAVE RECEIVED AND COUNTED 20M+ VOTES BY 8:02PM OF MAY 9, 2022.

HERE IS A CASE IN POINT, where a precinct in Barayong Elementary School, Palo, Leyte, obviously closed some 10 minutes before the official closing time of 7pm. It was able to print its first ER at 7:02:42pm. Yet in the Reception Log shown by COMELEC in its website, this same ER containing the actual votes of 342 voters was received by the Transparency Server (TS) at 10:26:33pm, or more than 3 hours after the ER was printed. In most precincts in the rural areas, transmitting the ERs was a problem because of poor telco signals. But the same Reception Log showed several anomalies where the TS received the ERs several minutes, even hours, BEFORE these ERS were being printed.

That is why COMELEC must show the actual Transmission Logs, verified thru the Telcos CDRs, so that it can be compared with the Reception Logs it uploaded in its website which is full of anomalous data. It must stop deceiving the people that the Reception Logs are the same as the Transmission Logs. COMELEC had actually shown the Transmission Logs in a graph "Accumulated VCM Transmissions" on October 18, 2022 which PEAKED at the SECOND HOUR after transmissions started, in stark contrast with with Transparency Server received data that PEAKED at the FIRST HOUR after voting closed.

IN A CLEAN AND HONEST ELECTION, THE VCM TRANSMISSION LOGS MUST MATCH THE RECEPTION LOGS OF THE TRANSPARENCY SERVER. IF IT DOES NOT, THEN THE 2022 ELECTION WAS RIGGED, NO MATTER HOW ACCURATE THE RESULTS OBSERVED BY SO-CALLED WATCHDOGS MAY SAY.

(comments)

Ronnie Adriano Amoroso
From 19.08.50 hours To 20.02.00 hours, May/9/2022:
# of Transmissions Received, VCM = 39,512 VCMs
# of Transmissions Received, Votes = 20,676,880 Votes
EXPLAIN, IPAKITA MO COMELEC ANG PROOF = TRUE VCM TRANSMISSION LOGS, ETC.

Ronnie Adriano Amoroso

DECEPTION LOGS, DECEPTION SERVERS, DECEPTION LAHAT.....

Ronnie Adriano Amoroso
LIARS DECEIVERS COM COMMI GEG ET. AL. STOP YOUR LIES DECEPTIONS.
  ○   **Like**

Ronnie Adriano Amoroso
LAPSED NA PO, PRESCRIBED NA PO, ANG PERIOD TO FILE ELECTION PROTEST.

Ronnie Adriano Amoroso
Deception #4. IRREGULARITIES observed and reported to Comelec BEFORE the May 9, 2022 NLE, and blatantly IGNORED/DISREGARDED by Comelec, are the MOST DAMNING OF ALL !!! The RIGGING WAS DONE PERVASIVELY - before, during and after that fateful date May 9, 2022. TAE NA x 100 !!!

oooooo

13
BEYOND TRILLANES' S SURVEYS: TNTrio's TECHNICAL ANALYSIS OF THE ELECTORAL FRAUD - sharing a post of Tina A. Astorga: - May 2023

BEYOND TRILLANES' S SURVEYS: TNTrio's TECHNICAL ANALYSIS OF THE ELECTORAL FRAUD
The International Observers Mission reported the massive vote buying in its findings and analysis of Elections 2022. It declared that Marcos and Duterte were illegitimately elected, and that Elections 2022 failed

the Filipino people. This was confirmed by the results of the investigation of the TNTrio of the ACTUAL ELECTION DATA. They ripped into the data using their expertise as IT, and found DIRECT EVIDENCE OF FRAUD, besides the preponderance of circumstantial evidence. So besides the massive vote buying, the ACTUAL ELECTION DATA were manipulated.

Trillanes is using the survey results as a basis of his declaration that there was no electoral fraud. But surveys are different from the ACTUAL ELECTION DATA. He could not conclude that there is no electoral fraud simply because the Magdalo survey coincided with the results of the Election. At this point, we have to rely on what actually happened with the election data, beyond surveys.

If there is DIRECT EVIDENCE OF FRAUD, then the ELECTION is illegitimate. TNTRio has in fact demonstrated the direct evidence of fraud, using the data of Comelec itself. They saw that the Transparency Server was already posting data which the VCMs from the precincts had not yet transmitted. It is like your friend receiving a message which you have not yet sent through your cel phone. There was one case where results were already posted on the Transparency Server 2 hours before the VCM transmission. The machine cannot do this on its own; someone manipulated the system.

May we ask Sen. Trillanes to stop making public declarations that there has been no electoral fraud, while TNTRio is fighting for the full integrity of Elections 2022.. May he allow the complete truth to come out? And may he be open to the findings of the TNTrio, who, as the IT experts, have the tools to examine the ACTUAL ELECTION DATA.

Hindi na pinaguusapan ang surveys dito; It is now technical analysis of the fraud in the electoral process itself.

PLEASE SIGN THE PEOPLE' MANDAMUS TO COMPEL COMELEC TO PUBLISH THE TRUE TRANSMISSION LOGS. You do not need to chip in money. PLEASE PIN THIS POST ON YOUR WALL, and ask your family, friends, associates, your entire network of contacts, to sign. As of now we have only 19k signatures. We need 100k signatures and more to support our petition in the SC to compel Comelec to do its constitutional duty.

https://m.facebook.com/story.php?story_fbid=7258026320880787&id=100000204740804&mibextid=Nif5oz

Please click this link NOW and sign:

oooooo

14
Impeach by People Power - Santos Aljo – May 1, 2023

Just MaryKaye 🌸 @karenvaughn_ · 12h
Breaking‼️
Ung prayer vigil s harap ng Comelec.Hndi po un rally!
Eto na ang pnka-hihintay ntin 👆 Kakampink: ayon kay Col. Odoño,mgka2roon tau ng mlwkang rally na ta2wagin nting #ArawNgDayaan sa May 9.Pupunta ang mga ex- militar at CBCP,at mga iba ibang grupo kya mghanda na!
CTTO

The National Statistics office reports that the number of voters in the Philippines was posted at 43,331,229 persons or 56.64 percent of the total population.

The 2022 elections showed an unexplained increase of 60% casted votes or a total of 19 million more ballots reported who allegedly voted.
NSO/ COMELEC Registered VOTERS = 44 Million
Actually read by smartmatic machines/unofficial = 61 million votes.
Over voted = 18 million extra.

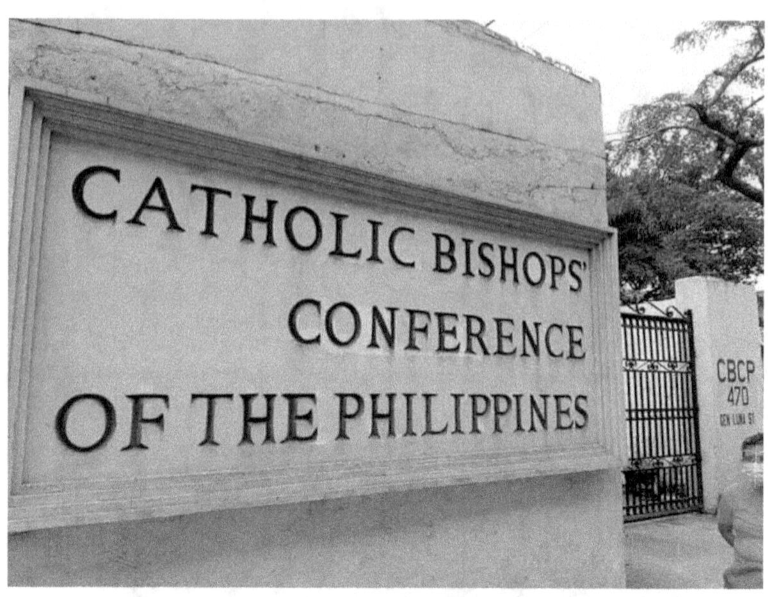

CATHOLIC BISHOPS'
CONFERENCE
OF THE PHILIPPINES
CBCP
470
GEN LUNA ST

The CAVALIER
COURAGE ★ INTEGRITY ★ LOYALTY
Publication of the Philippine Military Academy Alumni Association, Inc.
January–February 2018
FORT GEN GREGORIO H. DEL PILAR
INTEGRITY
Back to the PORTALS
of the ACADEMY
THE CAVALIER MAGAZINE

Santos Alio Posting

FILIPINO KANG GALIT sa 'pandaraya, kasinungalingan, panloloko, kawalanghiyaan ng mga 'kawatan: Tara na sa Prayer Vigil infront of the COMELEC - Commission On Election office in the Spanish walled city of Intramuros, Manila, come May 09,2023, LETS GO !. SEE 1st photo below,

FYI: Bakit Marcos palagi "nakikinabang sa mga elections na may dayaan", BAKIT ?.

DURING PBBMarcos Jr. "father's time of Conjugal Dictatorship from January 1/65 to February 25/86 = 20 yrs. & 55 days: ex-PFEMarcos Sr's COMELEC Officials "cheated in favor of their 'boss Apo Ferdie Marcos "beyond reasonable doubt !..

TODAY: With ex-PRRD30 "appointed COMELEC officials; General Eliseo Rio Jr./TNTrio had "proven beyond reasonable doubt too that "20 million questionable votes 'made the D30 "supported Unity party w/ BBMarcos Jr. & daughter SaraD30 as "standards bearers won.

PANAHON NA NG PAGKAKAISA(again): Come May 09,2023 a prayer vigil = time of being awake to pray(like the 3 days EDSA People Power Vigil of Feb.22

to 25,1986) at the COMELEC Office in Intramuros, Manila, LETS GO ! : TAP Virni Lisa's "Magkaisa": https://m.youtube.com/watch?v=Cq-5K5f3yuw&feature=share..

.

HISTORY IS BEING REPEATED: Our World Renowned EDSA People Power 'Bloodless Revolution of February 22-25,1986 was "sparked by the 'cheating of ex-PFEMarcos Sr. COMELEC during the February 07,1986 election. Then Defense Secretary JPEnrile(a certified balimbing=double faced) & PC/INP Chief General Fidel Valdez Ramos were 'disgusted, denied support & broke away from the "bogus gov't. of PFEMarcos Sr.

EVENTUALLY; Julio Cardinal Sin as Arcbishop of Manila of the CBCP - Catholic Bishop Conference of the PH in Feb.22/86 "through Radyo Bandido - DZRJ "called for the Filipino people to "protect GFVRamos & SJPEnrile "holed up" at Campo Crame, QC from Marcos: TAP to confirm; https://fb.watch/k8AP5PUYpa/

FIRST to "respond was the ATOM - August Twenty One Movement "led by SNinoy Aquino's brother Butz Aquino, Senator Tito Guingona & friends. TAP to confirm:
https://m.facebook.com/photo.php?fbid=1015366262
8403267&id=787063266&set=a.1066667368266

TODAY: General Eliseo Trio Jr. son of Col. Eliseo Rio Sr. of PMA Class 42', TNTrio, plus "active & retired military personnel like Colonel Leonardo Odono of PMA Class 64'(retired) & Col. Dencio Acop of USMA - US Military Academy of West Point New York,USA Class 83' - PMA Class 83(retired) their 'mistahs, active PMA Cavaliers & graduates are also "protesting these "cheating 'beyond reasonable doubt during the May 09,2022 elections.

TAP related articles,

(1) FACTS about the EDSA People Power Revolution of February 22 to 25,1986:

https://m.facebook.com/story.php?story_fbid=18350
4061289824&id=100088906935366

(2) HISTORY being repeated ?; (a)
https://m.facebook.com/story.php?story_fbid=16440
7953199435&id=100088906935366 (b)
https://m.facebook.com/story.php?story_fbid=17132
5872507643&id=100088906935366

(3) May 09,2022: Rigged beyond reasonable
doubt by General Rio Jr.;
https://m.facebook.com/story.php?story_fbid=17122
5709184326&id=100088906935366

(4) MAGKANONG Dahilan for COMELEC
Officials to cheat;
https://m.facebook.com/story.php?story_fbid=18075
0494898514&id=100088906935366

(5) LANDSLIDE Victory of PBBMarcos Jr. &
VPSaraD30 "bogus ?:
https://m.facebook.com/story.php?story_fbid=18205
0668101830&id=100088906935366

* PLEASE SHARE: So every Filipino must know;
that "dishonesty & cheating is "never acceptable to
'decent, God fearing Pinoys..

oooooo

15
Duterte -
Tommy Tongson – May 1, 2023
(facebook posting)

"a nation can survive its fools, and even the ambitious. but it cannot survive treason from within. an enemy at the gates is less formidable, for he is known and carries his banner openly. but the traitor moves amongst those within the gate freely, his sly whispers

rustling through all the alleys, heard in the very halls of government itself......." marcus tullius cicero

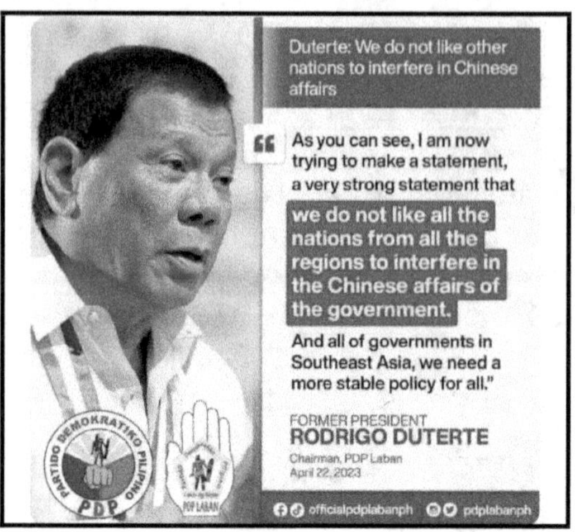

<u>Logie Kinko</u>

Why is the Philippine Republic bending over backward to protect Rodrigo Duterte? Why are top government Officials scrambling to defend him? Duterte does not deserve any defense from anyone. Least of all the entire country. Let's not forget Duterte himself never lifted a finger to defend the Philippines and her people. He was only too happy to cede our sovereign waters to China. He never invoked the UNCLOS ruling that demarcated internationally established exclusive zones. It was a landmark ruling that could've compelled China to abandon their encroachment. Instead Duterte shelved the ruling, didn't even use it as leverage for negotiation, and even floated the idea that China should make us a province of theirs. Of course that last bit is being dismissed as a crude joke. But joke or not, the fact that he sat on the UNCLOS ruling and allowed China complete liberty in our waters makes his inaction highly suspect.

Let's be truthful here. Duterte never put the interests of the country first and foremost. And from the historical record of his presidency, it's doubtful that he actually considered national interests at all. During his entire term, he ingratiated himself to China and he made crucial decions based solely on his desire to satisfy the Chinese. At the start of the pandemic, he chose to protect Chinese sensibilities over Filipino lives and refused to seal our borders to their travellers. He insisted on the inferior and more expensive Chinese vaccine. He preferred Chinese loans at usurious rates and with added conditions of hiring their workers. He allowed POGOs to proliferate without paying taxes and welcomed all the nefarious characters associated with their operations. His tenacious defense of the Pharmally scammers was done despite all evidence of guilt. Without fail he always gave consideration to the Chinese at the expense of the Filipinos.

But that's not all. Duterte's apparent loyalty to Chinese interests isn't the only factor why he deserves no quarter from the Filipino nation. Mainly because he gave no quarter to Filipinos. For someone who repeatedly claimed to love the Philippines, he showed a remarkable hatred of Filipinos. He ordered the murder of tens of thousands without due process. He cursed the poverty stricken masses when they resisted his Jeepney modernization program. He corrupted the police organization by insisting that they practice vigilante justice (he even coached them on planting evidence) and even gave them a personal guarantee that none of them will be prosecuted as long as he was president.

Still, Duterte's transgressions to the country and its people did not end there. His arrogant, childish, abrasive behavior was an embarrassment to the flag. He cussed and swore at world dignitaries including Pres Obama, Colombian president Gaviria, and the Pope, hurling all manner of insults at them. Not content with world leaders, the asshole even called God stupid. He traveled to Israel on a diplomatic mission only to be lectured by the Prime Minister then sent home in rejection. He was refused an audience with the Jordanian King because of his slight of the King's cousin. He was notorious for his crude behavior that he was treated as a pariah in all international summits he attended. Largely ignored by world leaders and only greeted as a curiosity. A simpleton, troglodyte who somehow infiltrated the halls of power.

Of course his defenders have always dismissed his rhetoric as mere jokes. Unfunny as they were, they weren't meant as policy. What they all fail to acknowledge is that being the leader of the country, every word out of his mouth WAS deemed as policy. But more compelling than that, everything he "joked" about actually came to pass. Killings actually skyrocketed; the police actually planted evidence; the Chinese ran roughshod over our waters; and the country descended into a morass of murder, corruption, indecency, and immorality.

And it was all because of this foul-mouthed, malbred, gutter minded, pond scum of a man. Duterte will go down in history as certainly the worst president of the country to date. He is probably among the worst Filipinos of his generation. A man who inherited a robust economy plus P1T and turned it into an P11T national debt in a span of 6 years. This man's crimes will trouble the Filipinos for generations to come. He deserves no defense from the people. In fact, he should be served up to the ICC in a silver platter. He doesn't deserve the allegiance of a country he never gave his allegiance to.

oooooo

16

Comelec Deletes backup files used in May 9 polls - Mhel Mendez Bulabos – May 2023

Grievous and severe crime was committed by the Comelec against the Filipino people by this odious and blatant act of omission.

Mhel Mendez Bulabos
Namfrel's IT team noticed something wrong during Comelec's end-to-end demonstration of the

election system on Mar. 22, 2022: "The VCM System Hash Code shown during the demo did not match what was published during the second Final Trusted Build." The process of building components into a system, which included the generation of the system hash, was never shown publicly. Aside from the VCM System Hash, no other hash codes were shared for public check," Namfrel concluded. "Without the system hash generation in full view of stakeholders, the source code that Namfrel saw and reviewed could be different from what was used by the VCMs on Election Day. In layman terms, this software used on the VCMs on Election Day … could have been edited."

Jun Camat
COMELEC IS GUILTY BEYOND REASONABLE DOUBT!

Romeo Velasco
That is one big issue on May 9 rally to puff up why they(comelec) deleted at once that very important record.They should be made to explain to the fil people.They did that deletion for an obvious reasons.They are traitors that deserve punishment

Nestor Marcelo
Comelec is Guilty!

Jose Chua
tampering of evidence is a big crime
the DOJ if still honest should take a look
lock them up…

Evangeline Dare
With this kind of news headline, it's a puzzle why there were no reverberations at all from the public or from opinion makers.
Ooooooo

No.

A PLEA FOR DELICADEZA from the involved COMELEC Commissioners and their Chairman to INHIBIT THEMSELVES from now on during EN BANC DECISIONS regarding our DEMAND FOR TRUTH AND TRANSPARENCY concerning the 2022 National Elections: - Lourdes Hipolito (Ason Hipolito)

28 April 2023

Chairman George Erwin Mojica Garcia
Commissioner Socorro Balinghasay Inting
Commissioner Marlon Sabucido Casquejo
Commissioner Aimee Ferolino Ampoloquio
Commissioner Rey Echavarria Bulay
Commissioner Nelson Java Celis
Commissioner Ernesto Vera Perez Maceda
COMMISSION ON ELECTIONS (COMELEC)
<clerkofthecommission@comelec.gov.ph>
Palacio del Gobernador Building ‹ Intramuros ‹ Manila

Your Honors:

This is a follow-up to my earlier constitutional-right-to-know and freedom of information (FOI) request for **Transmission** Data Logs = not **Reception** Data Logs such as the one given to me last 23 March 2023. No less than the COMELEC website expressly labels it as the "List of VCM **Received** Transmission Logs". Hence the time stamps there report the time of **receipt** by the Central Server instead of the more important time of **transmission** by the vote counting machines or VCM nationwide. The said 23 March 2023 reception data logs contain numerous embarrassments such as the significant number of VCM transmission reports with time stamps reporting transmission times that came **after** (instead of before) their respective reception time by the Central Server and/or Transparency Server.

I therefore respectfully request for a simple win-win compromise solution by just simply allowing the telecommunication companies (DITO Tele-community & Globe Telecom & Smart Communications) to disclose their copies of the very same data that is the subject matter of this lawful request for the People.

I likewise respectfully request for *delicadeza* in the resolution of this request. Undeniably, the COMELEC Chairman and the first four Commissioners cannot resolve this request with cold impartial neutrality. The said Chairman and first four Commissioners must therefore voluntarily inhibit from the En Banc deliberation for the approval or disapproval of this request. *Delicadeza* voluntary inhibitions by five-out-of-seven in the En Banc may result to apparent lack of quorum but that is not a problem because the Administrative Code provides for a solution wherein the COURT OF APPEALS (CA) Presiding Justice shall designate a CA Justice or CA Justices who shall join Commissioner Nelson Java Celis and Commissioner Ernesto Vera Perez Maceda in constituting a special quorum that shall resolve the particularly specific issue pertaining to transmission versus reception data logs. Please refer to the Administrative Code specifically in (Book V) (Title I = Constitutional Commissions) (Sub-Title C = COMELEC) (Chapter 2 = En Banc) (Section 6).

Cordially

Colonel **Leonardo** Olivera **Odoño** (retired)
Philippine Military Academy Class of 1964
<colloo64@yahoo.com>

Copy sent to the COURT OF APPEALS Presiding Justice
<coc.ca@judiciary.gov.ph>

---

28 April 2023
Chairman George Erwin Mojica Garcia

Commissioner Socorro Balinghasay Inting
Commissioner Marlon Sabucido Casquejo
Commissioner Aimee Ferolino Ampoloquio
Commissioner Rey Echavarria Bulay
Commissioner Nelson Java Celis
Commissioner Ernesto Vera Perez Maceda
COMMISSION ON ELECTIONS (COMELEC)
<clerkofthecommission@comelec.gov.ph>
Palacio del Gobernador Building < Intramuros <
Manila

Your Honors:
This is a follow-up to my earlier constitutional-right-to-know and freedom of information (FOI) request for Transmission Data Logs = not Reception Data Logs such as the one given to me last 23 March 2023. No less than the COMELEC website expressly labels it as the "List of VCM Received Transmission Logs". Hence the time stamps there report the time of receipt by the Central Server instead of the more important time of transmission by the vote counting machines or VCM nationwide. The said 23 March 2023 reception data logs contain numerous embarrassments such as the significant number of VCM transmission reports with time stamps reporting transmission times that came after (instead of before) their respective reception time by the Central Server and/or Transparency Server.

I therefore respectfully request for a simple win-win compromise solution by just simply allowing the telecommunication companies (DITO Tele-community & Globe Telecom & Smart Communications) to disclose their copies of the very same data that is the subject matter of this lawful request for the People.

I likewise respectfully request for delicadeza in the resolution of this request. Undeniably, the COMELEC Chairman and the first four Commissioners cannot
resolve this request with cold impartial neutrality. The

said Chairman and first four Commissioners must therefore voluntarily inhibit from the En Banc deliberation for the approval or disapproval of this request. Delicadeza

voluntary inhibitions by five-out-of-seven in the En Banc may result to apparent lack of quorum but that is not a problem because the Administrative Code provides for a solution wherein the COURT OF APPEALS (CA) Presiding Justice shall designate a CA Justice or CA Justices who shall join Commissioner Nelson Java Cells and Commissioner Ernesto Vera Perez Maceda in constituting a special quorum that shall resolve the particularly specific issue pertaining to transmission versus reception data logs. Please refer to the Administrative Code specifically in (Book V) (Title I = Constitutional Commissions) (Sub-Title C = COMELEC) (Chapter 2 = En Banc) (Section 6).

Cordially

Colonel Leonardo Olivera Odono (retired)
Philippine Military Academy Class of 1964
<colloo64@yahoo.com>

Copy sent to the Court of Appeals Presiding Justice
<coc.ca@judiciary.gov.ph>

Lourdes Hipolito

A PLEA FOR DELICADEZA from the involved COMELEC Commissioners and their Chairman to INHIBIT THEMSELVES from now on during EN BANC DECISIONS regarding our DEMAND FOR TRUTH AND TRANSPARENCY concerning the 2022 National Elections:

HEED the PLEA IF YOU ARE NOT GUILTY!!! ASON HIPOLITO

(comments)
Beth Flora
Thank God for you, Col Leonardo O Odoño (Ret), and Atty Mel Magdamo.

God give you the strength, courage, and wisdom to fight for truth, transparency, and justice which the Filipinos so deserve!

God bless you more abundantly

oooooo

17
IT Forensics & audit trail
fake election, fake government
– Franklin Ysaac -
posted by Lyndon Crisostomo
at fb – May 2023

Let me cut this whole matter of fraudulent results into this scenario which I described last year and which was validated by the expose of my colleague Eli Rio:

1. Smartmatic provided the automated election system which is a seamless process or straight through processing from casting of ballot, to counting , to printing of election returns and transmission reports.

2. The automated election system was witnessed by independent IT and was presumed to be perfect .

3. During the actual automated election process, the system was cut into parts which overrode the approved automated system.

4. The ERs were produced and the transmission reports were made.

5. The ERs and Transmission reports were given to political parties and ppcrv. The political parties kept the ERs but did not keep the transmission reports. These transmission reports eventually faded as the papers used were thermal paper.

6. We asked for copies of these transmission reports but we were ignored.

7. The ERs were eventually transmitted via telcos and were recorded under call detail reports.

8. We filed mandamus before SC to preserve the election data . Response was moot because they published the transmission logs.

9. We filed supplemental petition because the published transmission logs were not true and they were merely reception logs.

10. The whole process which was supposed to be seamless or straight through never happened. The ERs time logs do not reflect the same time logs even in reception logs. The ERs were transmitted much much later than the published reception logs giving rise to falsification of data.

11. The time logs from VCMs via Telco to Transparency server are supposed to be synchronized.

13. But what happened to the election data which passed through telcos but didn't end up in the transmission servers?

My judgment as IT is where is the real server or transparency server ?

In my Fb post last year, I mentioned that there is a strong possibility there are at least two transparency servers. One which is pre loaded and another which is the true transparency server ?

Questions:

A.Where are these data which were supposed to be transmitted by telco to the real server?

B. Who ordered the changes

In the automated system which is apparently not a seamless or straight through processing system ?

C. It the changes showed the apparent and perhaps deliberate attempt to change the results of the election, then those officials responsible have committed a serious crime?

We are closely studying this case and we will discuss this with our lawyers to make our case credible and irrefutable.

oooooo

18
US Filipinos For Good Governance – May 3, 2023

USFGG Statement on the Biden-Marcos White House meetings

We, the leaders of the US Filipinos for Good Governance advocacy group, hope President Biden will counsel President Marcos Jr. to release former Senator Leila De Lima from six years of political imprisonment and to be serious in upholding human rights and rule of law in the Philippines. This includes discussing the rights and welfare of the thousands of abandoned Amerasian children of US military fathers as part of the EDCA terms of engagement.

We will be disappointed with President Biden if he fails to stress his "human rights" concerns that he raised previously with Marcos Jr. during their September meeting in New York. Biden has pledged promotion of democracy as a priority of his administration.

We are anxious and conflicted about Biden's welcome for Marcos Jr. to the White House in light of his father's and mother's corrupt dictatorship in the 1970s and 80s. Bongbong Marcos Jr., as the executor of the estate of his father, still faces the Hawaii US Court judgment of $353 million in penalties to be paid to human rights victims and their families as well as the $3.6 billion in unpaid taxes and penalties to the Philippine Government.

Biden's officials should suggest to Marcos Jr. to settle these court cases to improve his family's reputation in the US Congress, where the Philippines will have a clearly difficult time getting additional military and economic aid.

With the USFGG Board of Directors
- Eric Lachica
Coordinator, Washington DC
US Filipinos for Good Governance, Inc.
#FreeLeilaNow

oooooo

19
Reminder from Col. Leonardo O. Odono (Ret.) about non-partisan nature of TNTRIO Movement for Truth – May 2023

SMART · 78% · 3:03

← ☰ TNTrio Mo... 🔍 ➤

Leonardo Odono

May I remind our Comrades that from the beginning, we your leaders have agreed, and decided, that our search for the truth behind the ugly results of the last election is to be, non-partisan, totally apolitical.. The purity, the nobility of our purpose and intentions - to bring out the truth and the truth alone - must not be tainted with any shade of political color. By nature, crises bring out a leader that circumstances call for. Let us wait for that to happen - by God's will.

The one thing thar can bring our movement to self-destruction is when the people we serve start suspecting, and believing we are doing what we are doing for an individual or a group to promote their personal interests. We will lose their support.

So, please, let us stop bugging Ms. Leni to come to our rallies, or speak in public in support of our cause, FOR NOW, There will be time for that, promise.

 Luv u all. Col. Leonardo O. Odoño (Ret.)

6h   Love   Reply   3 ◎◎

Rules

oooooo

20
Random Posters by all TNTRIO Movement Members

" COMELEC IS DECEIVING NOT ONLY THE VOTING PUBLIC BUT EVEN THE SUPREME COURT!" Ret. Brig. Gen Eliseo Rio, Jr.

We reached 10 k. We are now moving to a new goal 15 k. Please just sign the People's Mandamus. You do not need to contribute money. Keep signing. Click here: https://chng.it/79gg9SqWmq

As soon as we hit 1% or 500,000 signatures, we will append this number to our SC mandamus! They bear your names!

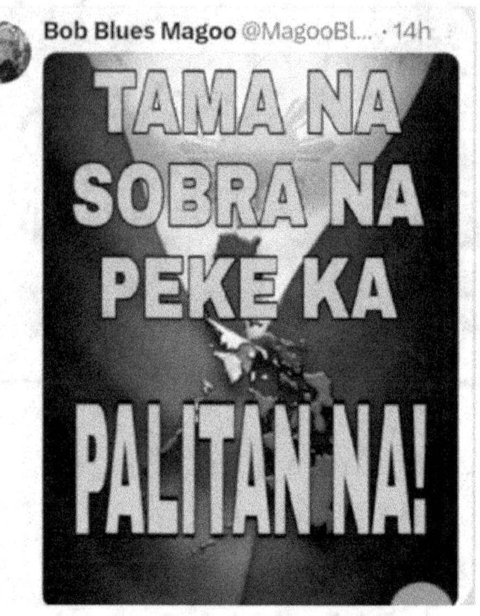
Bob Blues Magoo @MagooBl... · 14h
TAMA NA
SOBRA NA
PEKE KA
PALITAN NA!

Advisory 4: any Donation
should go only to our treasurer
Cristy M gcash and not to
People's Mandamus Change
org donation!

Without the TNTrio, we
would have been bereft of
hope. They are our three
wise men. We thank you. We
salute you.

You can share the fb People's
Mandamus to all your friends
after you sign up!

Ito sinasabi ko na sa inyo
ha, si Leni Robredo talaga
ang mananalong
Presidente... pero dadayain!

-Percy Lapid

The failure of Comelec
to meet the deadline
imposed by the SC is
repugnant. It is a lower
institution defying the
highest court of the
land. The SC should
render a default
judgment & proceed
with the case without
Comelec's
participation.

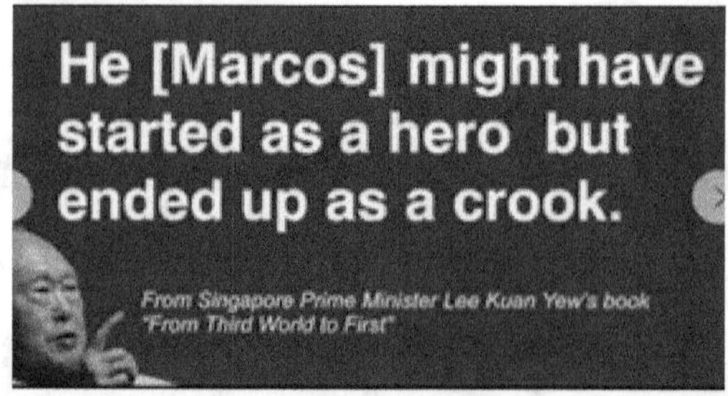

He [Marcos] might have started as a hero but ended up as a crook.
From Singapore Prime Minister Lee Kuan Yew's book "From Third World to First"

"The evidence is overwhelming...Marcos, Jr. and Sara Duterte were not elected legitimately."
—Lee Rhiannon, Member of the International Observers Mission (IOM)

"Mahirap kayo? Putangina, magtiis kayo sa hirap at gutom, wala akong pakialam!"
- President Rodrigo Roa Duterte -

"I will be the new SATAN"
- President Duterte
August 4, 2016 Speech
Malacanang Palace
BANTAY NAKAW

BBM
FOR PRESIDENT

T RODRIGO
DUTERTE TO SUPPORTERS:
I'LL WAIT FOR YOU IN HELL
one STAR

Philippine Presidential and Topnotcher-Senator Historical Scores

Year	President	Score	Senator	Score
1992	Ramos	5M	Sotto	11M
1998	Estrada	10M	Legarda	14M
2004	Arroyo	12M	Roxas	19M
2010	Aquino	15M	Revilla	19M
2016	Duterte	16M	Drilon	18M
2022	Marcos	31M	Robin	26M

1. Sa kasaysayan, laging MAS MATAAS ang bilang ng boto ng topnotcher na Senador kumpara sa nanalong Pangulo.

2. KAKAIBA ang "INCREASE" ng mga BOTANTE para sa taong 2022 kumpara sa mga nagdaang taon.

Comelec, respond to the mandamus! Sobrang sobra na ang delay. Ano ba kayo? Mga manloloko! Mga sindikato?

The more this govt publishes statements not backed up by truth, the more they are building a preponderance of lies!

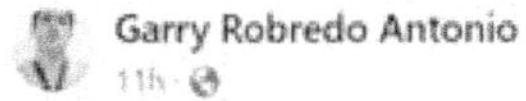

From a very reliable source:
Na-hacked na ng USA at Canada ang totoong results ng 2022 Philippine Presidential Elections. Robredo 39M, Marcos 14M.
No. 1 Senator is Delima, 2nd is Trillanes. Brace yourself!

Advisory 2: Naka pin na po ang Change org People's Mandamus to compel Comelec to disclose true transmission logs !

Eliseo Rio Jr
9m · 🌐

IT IS IMPOSSIBLE for a Server to receive data from a VCM BEFORE that VCM could transmit that data even for a split second.

Franklin Ysaac
3h · 🌐   ··· ✕

After mainstream media picked up questionable TL raised by concerned citizens, senate hearings may soon be conducted !!!

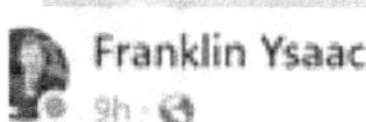

Franklin Ysaac
9h · 🌐

Thank you Lord for you have spoken through your people's mandamus and it has just breached the 3k mark already!

From TNTrio, thank you to all our followers! Truth is gaining traction ! Go spread the truth as the Truth is the Lord Himself!!

#SupportTNTrio
TNTrio MANDAMUS Petition
COMELEC
20+ MILLION VOTES
?
THE MAGICIANS OF THE PHILIPPINES
Do the right thing, even when no one is looking. It's called integrity.
SUPREME COURT
#NasaanAngBatasSaPilipinas

TRUTH is TREASON
in the EMPIRE of LIES.
LIES
truth
Kahit sa balumbon
ng sandamakmak
na kasinungalingan,
panlilinlang,
pandaraya at mga
fake news ay may
isang lalabas at
lalabas na
KATOTOHANAN.
ctto

KORONANG PEKE?!
IPINUTONG SA ULO...?
MALAMAFIANG PALACE
MANILA
PHILIPPI

Thank you to all who signed up in our People's Mandamus! In one and a half days, we breached 5k mark!Share pa More tayo !

Last year, I wrote in this fb about my dream encounter with Him and I prayed to Him to guide us in this truth campaign! He did!

What kind of world do liars live in ? Heaven or Hell?

Filipinos here & abroad: Please sign the petition: "People's Mandamus to Compel Comelec to Disclose True Transmission Logs." Click https://chng.it/79gg9SqWmq

Prediction Dec. 2021

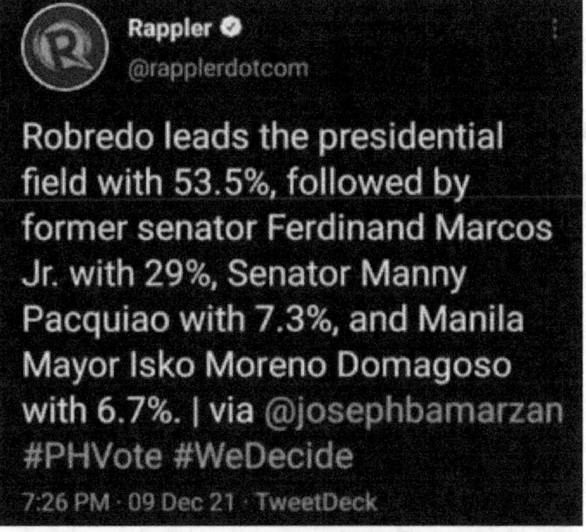

TELCOS your duty is to the Filipino people & not to COMELEC! Expose the truth through your transmission logs!

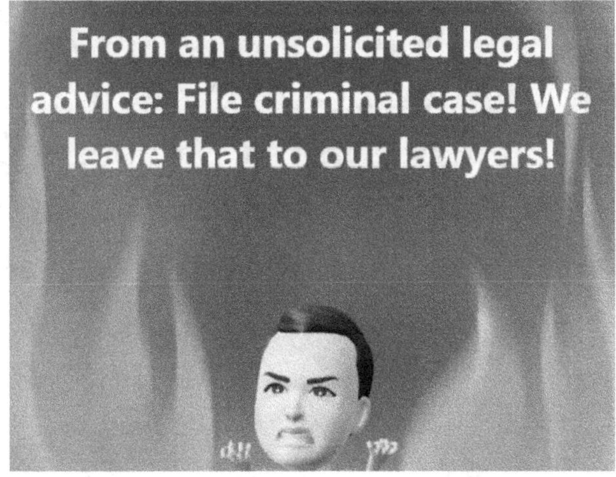

To subvert or sabotage a free and fair elections is criminal. File criminal case against saboteurs of the Filipino electoral will.

A PUBLIC APPEAL to VP LENI & All PATRIOTIC LEADERS! Please lead the People's Mandamus— the right of EVERY FILIPINO to an honest & fair elections. The MANDAMUS is beyond political color! It protects the SOUL of our democracy!

And let us not forget to pray— to storm the heavens for divine intervention in and through the confluence of persons & events. Tutumbok at tutumbok ang mga pangyayari! We need our prayer warriors!

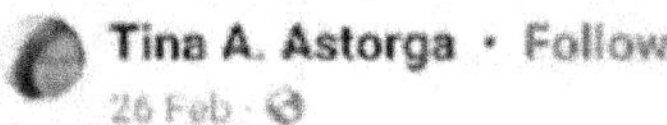

Tina A. Astorga · Follow
26 Feb · 🌐

"The evidence is
overwhelming...Marcos, Jr.
and Sara Duterte were not
elected legitimately."
—Lee Rhiannon, Member
of the International
Observers Mission (IOM)

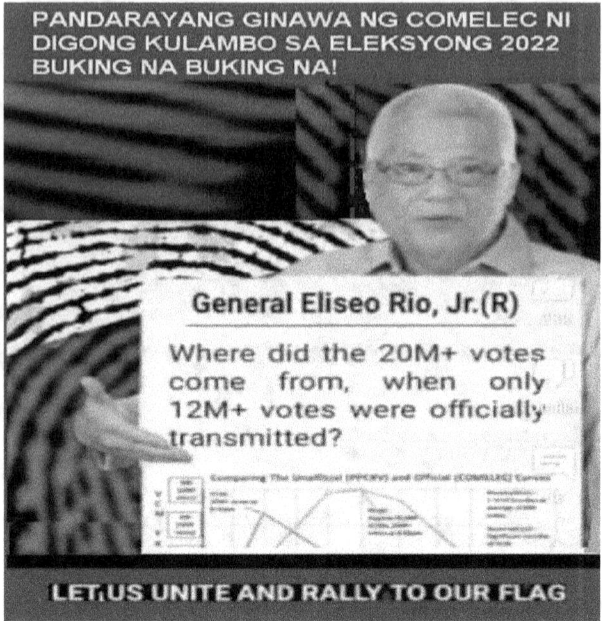

Our people's **MANDAMUS** is a petition to SC to command/compel a lower gov't agency (Comelec) to fulfill its duty— to disclose the transparency logs! Sign & skip donation:
https://chng.it/79gg9SqWmq

For months, nobody paid attention to TNTrio's search for truth. Now that they found it, they want to destroy the truth.

The trolls, fake news, vloggers, bloggers are back! Judases are few but they make lots of noises! Don't listen to them!

The trolls, fake news, vloggers, bloggers are back! Judases are few but they make lots of noises! Don't listen to them!

Divine Justice is the constant and unchanging will of God to give everyone what is due him or her!

Trolls are not IT experts !
They don't even know what
debug is?

To prove that election was not
fraudulent, let's repeat
election! This time, no
smartmatic, no ppcrv!Hybrid
tayo !

Inconsistency #1
20M+ votes counted
PEAKED at 1st hour
while VCM
transmissions PEAKED
at 2nd hour.

Rejoice in the triumphant
resurrection of Jesus but be
vigilant of the remaining
Judases who have no guilt!

Inconsistency #2
Making transmission logs
public will violate the
sanctity of the ballot yet
these were made public on
March 23.

Inconsistency #3
COMELEC said it will
make transmission
logs public but what it
published are
reception logs.

Every possible form of Justice
is possessed by God!

Viva Mighty Jesus !
Viva Mandamus
!
Viva Pilipino !

Finally, our lawyer will file supplemental petition to compel Comelec to release true TL after it bungled / showed irregular TL!

The TNTRio are not just citizens questioning the integrity of the elections. They are recognized IT experts with very impressive credentials.

On the COMELEC: "We know they are lying, they know they are lying, they know we know they are lying, we know they know we know they are lying, but they are still lying...."
Alexander Isayevich Solzhenitsyn

Let us pray fervently for our country, that crucified now, it may rise to new life, in Christ, through the intercession of Mother Mary.Amen.

The UP Vanguards for Truth and Transparency call
for peaceful public protests in support of the
impeachment of the Commissioners of COMELEC!
Please sign People's Mandamus. Click & sign:
https://chng.it/79gg9SqWmq

To win peace, you study, expose, defend against the trajectory of lies being hurled on ordinary people !

When this transmission log case is in court, no amount of false rhetorics can cover the respondents credibility!

For peace of mind, TNTrio is moving at a pace calculated to make a successful campaign amidst wrongful responses!

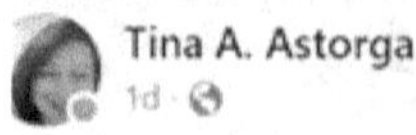

May the nation be set free from the throes of death to new life, new hope, new future, by the power & grace of the Risen Christ!

COMELEC's direct Act of Deception:

ANG HINIHINGI SA KANILA AY TRANSMISSION LOGS. ANG IBINIGAY NILA AY RECEPTION LOGS OF ELECTION/5/9/22

Malinaw na PANLOLOKO!

Da Celestine

The reason we brought the mandamus case to SC is because the respondents refuse to give us the truth! Under oath, they must!

Telco Subscribers: It's time to call out all the Telcos to disclose the Call Detail Records(CDRs) on VCM transmissions!

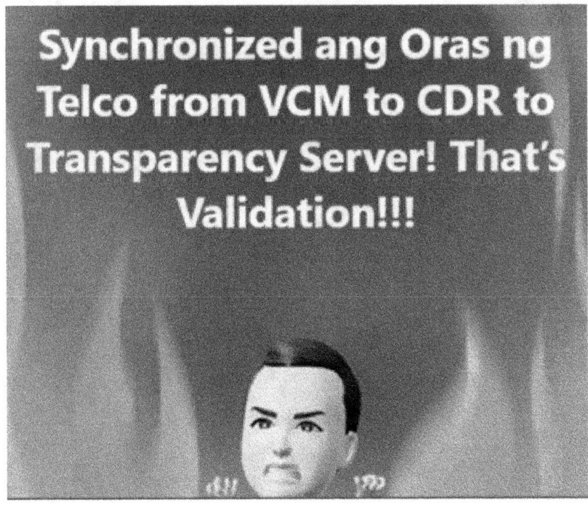
Synchronized ang Oras ng Telco from VCM to CDR to Transparency Server! That's Validation!!!

The reason we brought the mandamus case to SC is because the respondents refuse to give us the truth! Under oath, they must!

Telcos cannot invoke data privacy act(dpa) to keep CDRs. Dpa applies to individual protection not to govt .FOI is mandamus

Smartmatic is one of the respondents in our SC mandamus and it has not responded!

Telco Subscribers: It's time to call out all the Telcos to disclose the Call Detail Records(CDRs) on VCM transmissions!

SWITCHING THE REAL RESULTS OF VP LENI ROBREDO THROUGH PROGRAMMED COMPUTERS IS TREASON. COMELEC RESIGN!
Tayo na labanan natin sila!
HUWAG HA MATAKOT

Kapag na-IMPEACH ang mga COMELEC Commissioners, REPLACEMENT lang ang susunod na hakbang ng presidente.

Mas maganda kung kasabay ng COMELEC IMPEACHMENT ay mag-deklara ng FAILURE OF ELECTIONS at PATALSIKIN ang LAHAT ng PEKE.

SC ordered CAC and JCOAE, two bodies Comelec referred us to last year for TL, as respondents! No answer also !

Synchronized ang Oras ng Telco from VCM to CDR to Transparency Server! That's Validation!!!

BBM and Sara D are as eerily silent as Comelec in the face of the election fraud! Were they assured that it was foolproof and are now stunned into silence that it went ppfft!??

Telco Subscribers: It's time to call out all the Telcos to disclose the Call Detail Records(CDRs) on VCM transmissions!

Telcos cannot invoke data privacy act(dpa) to keep CDRs. Dpa applies to individual protection not to govt .FOI is mandamus

**Red tagging Sunday's online public forum exposes the desperate efforts of the true enemies of the people to derail
the fight for truth!**

One follower remarked: Our truth campaign is like a game of chess! You make the wrong move , you lose!

When this transmission log case is in court, no amount of false rhetorics can cover the respondents credibility!

Telcos should disclose CDRs: Comelec owns SIM, People pays Comelec who pays Telcos! People have right to know CDRs!

Smartmatic is one of the respondents in our SC mandamus and it has not responded!

Send email to President of Smart, Globe, Ditto to compel them to disclose CDRs of transmissions from VCMs!!!

Fighting for truth & justice is at the core of being Christian. It is the heart of the Gospel. To red tag fighters for truth & justice is diabolical. It is the work of evil.

And Comelec has the gall to ask for another round of billions to replace the VCMs of Smartmatic!

**SWS, Pulse Asia, Bbm trolls
They are being paid to spread
lies and fool the people
Kaya huwag paloko !**

Bukod sa COMMISSIONER,
mga DOKTOR din pala sila.
SAGRADONG BOTO NG MGA PILIPINO HILAPASTANGAN NG MGA SUKABI
OKAY NA, PWEDE NG ISA-
PUBLIKO YUNG DINOKTOR NATIN
NA TRANSMISSION LOGS
#Smartmagic
#HocusPocus
#TransmissionLogs
GEORGE GARCIA
AIMEE FEROLINO
NELSON CELIS
ERNESTO MACEDA JR.
SOCORRO INTING
MAY 9, 2022
TRANSMISSION LOGS
Dapat managot sa batas at sa taumbayan ang
mga dumoktor sa resulta at nag-moneypula
ng dayaan sa halalan noong May 9, 2022.

Truth #15

FRAUDULENT!!!

The May 2022 Election was RIGGED
from the very beginning!

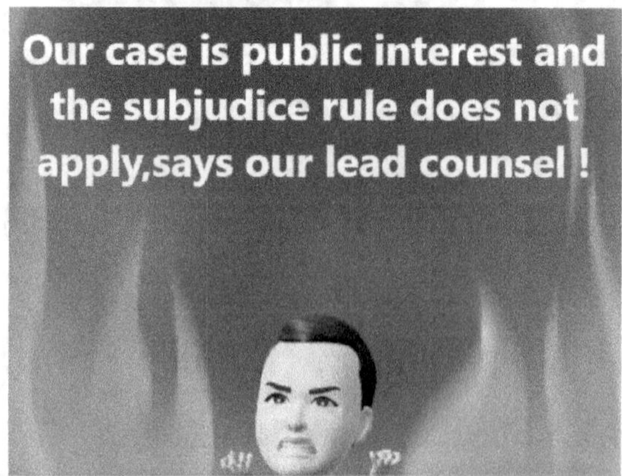
Our case is public interest and
the subjudice rule does not
apply,says our lead counsel !

The IT and company can be held responsible, accountable, and charged in court for fabricating evidence !
Coming out with false explanation outside the court instead of presenting it under oath in court does not make our case "moot"!

A cover-up or an attempt to prevent people's discovering the Truth about a serious mistake or crime is a crime!

Do dates have special meanings in history- April 9, we commemorate Death March / May 9, 2022 is Death of Democracy!

The IT and company can be held responsible, accountable, and charged in court for fabricating evidence !

Let us support the TNTrio on their fight for the Truth. Their Fight is OUR Fight God Bless Us All !

"Too big to fail"is not equivalent to "Too big to fall"!

To boost our Truth campaign, we call on all to sign on people's mandamus signature campaign which is pinned on this fb !

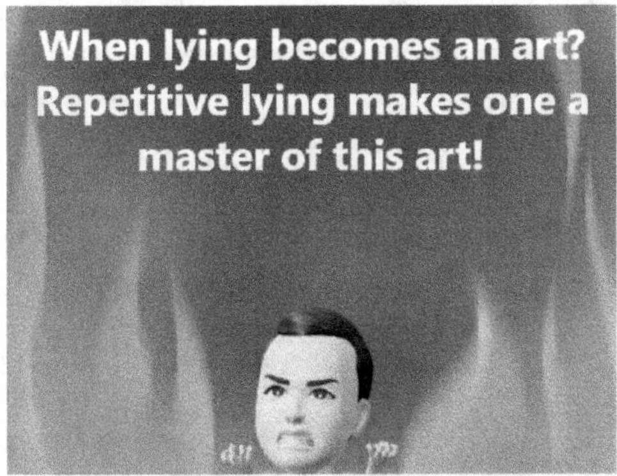
When lying becomes an art? Repetitive lying makes one a master of this art!

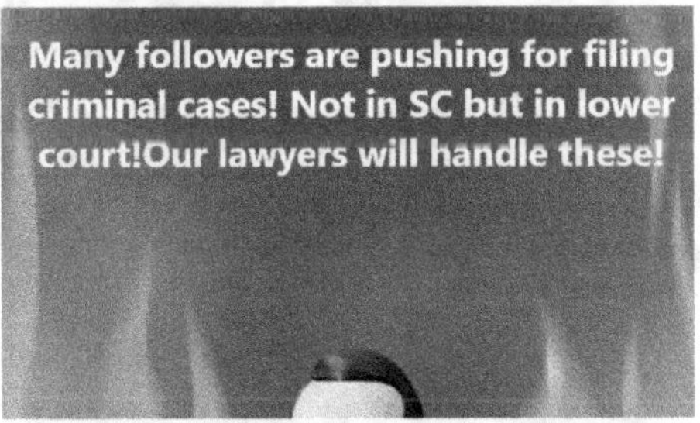
Many followers are pushing for filing criminal cases! Not in SC but in lower court!Our lawyers will handle these!

" Let Justice be done though heavens fall". Justice must be realized regardless of consequences !

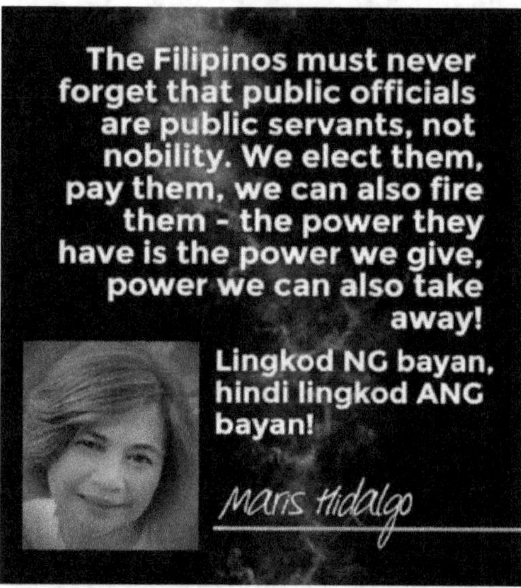
After our successful prayer rally before SC, we enjoin everyone to participate in our forthcoming prayer rallies!

The Filipinos must never forget that public officials are public servants, not nobility. We elect them, pay them, we can also fire them - the power they have is the power we give, power we can also take away!

Lingkod NG bayan, hindi lingkod ANG bayan!

Maris Hidalgo

The fight for truth is between the People of the Phils vs Govt! On Court or Off Court ! Join May 9 rally!!

Nakaktulog pa kaya ng mahimbing ang mga tao sa Comelec o puro mga binabangungot na? Sabagay kung sadyang makakapal na ang mukha ay di na tinatablan yan. Hayaan na lang nating karma ang humusga.
Many followers are pushing for filing criminal cases! Not in SC but in lower court!Our lawyers will handle these!
You can't trust a friend who lied to you once as he or she will be lying to you forever !

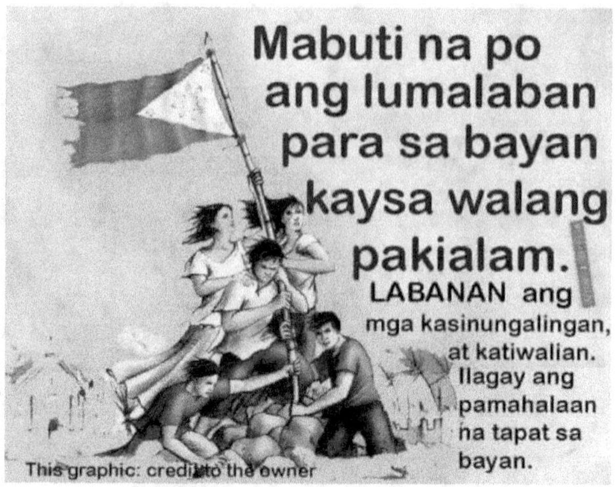
Mabuti na po ang lumalaban para sa bayan kaysa walang pakialam.
LABANAN ang mga kasinungalingan, at katiwalian. Ilagay ang pamahalaan ha tapat sa bayan.
This graphic: credit to the owner

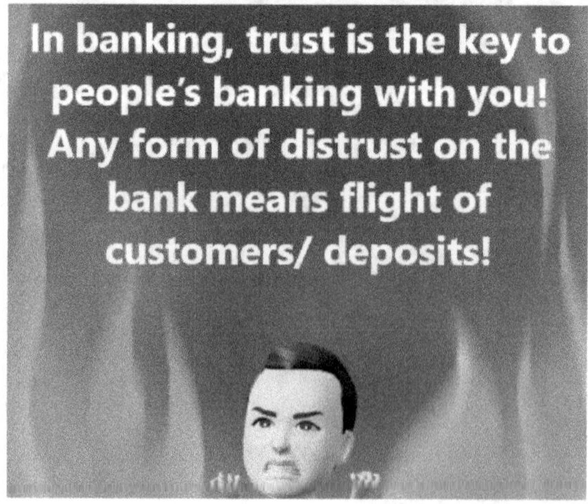
In my line of work, I learned not to trust anyone right away! My motto is " you are not trustworthy and you have to earn my trust "

In banking, trust is the key to people's banking with you! Any form of distrust on the bank means flight of customers/ deposits!

Transmission log is the Pandora's box in the May 9, 2022 election to which the Comelec is so afraid to open.

" Day of Reckoning " is May 9! Join the thousands and make our presence felt that they are not above the law!

Transmission log is the Pandora's box in the May 9, 2022 election to which the Comelec is so afraid to open.

Let us support the TNTrio on their fight for the Truth. Their Fight is OUR Fight God Bless Us All !

Signing the People's Mandamus is the barest minimum we can do for our nation. Please click this link Now & sign: https://chng.it/79gg9SqWmq. Please Share.

Signing the People's Mandamus is the barest minimum we can do for our nation. Please click this link Now & sign: https://chng.it/79gg9SqWmq. Please Share.

COMELEC Chairperson: Ang hinihingi po ng TNTrio ay picture pag take off ng Eroplano, hindi po picture pag Landing!

The machines could not on their own post votes on Transparency servers BEFORE they were transmitted by the VCMs. One does not receive a message BEFORE it was sent! Someone manipulated the system!

The Comelec transparency server posted votes which the VCMs of precincts have not yet transmitted. Like your friend posting your message which you have not yet sent. Miracle? No! Manipulation of the electoral system!

Fake surveys are back!Follow google trends and try reliable product survey co Nielsen which are true surveys!

IMPEACH THE ENTIRE COMELEC BETRAYAL OF PUBLIC TRUST

" Day of Reckoning " is May 9! Join the thousands and make our presence felt that they are not above the law!

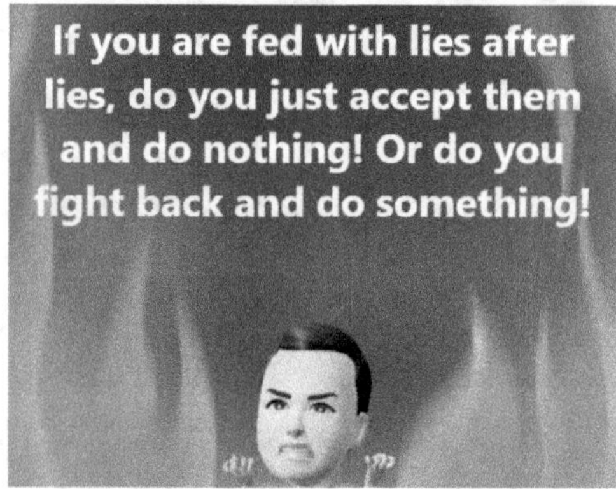
Magkaisa npo
tayong lahat sa
May 9 po isang
taon na ang dayaan
ipaglaban na natin
ang katotohanan,
ipakita natin muli ang
ating lakas gawin
natin muli ang
PEOPLE POWER

If you are fed with lies after
lies, do you just accept them
and do nothing! Or do you
fight back and do something!

After our novena which will
end on May 9, the day of
reckoning, we will make
another for release of Sen
Leila!

 Franklin Ysaac +

Eliseo Rio Jr. + Augusto Guzman

After a series of faux pas, the respondents and the institution they represent don't have the gravitas to redeem themselves!

Vcr
@vince2681
#ArawngDayaan

It's now a matter of time. 125+ retired AFP Senior Officers call on the COMOLEC to come clean. Jr & SWoH are getting nervous

The Transparency Server was counting more votes than what the VCMs were transmitting from 7:00–9:00PM.

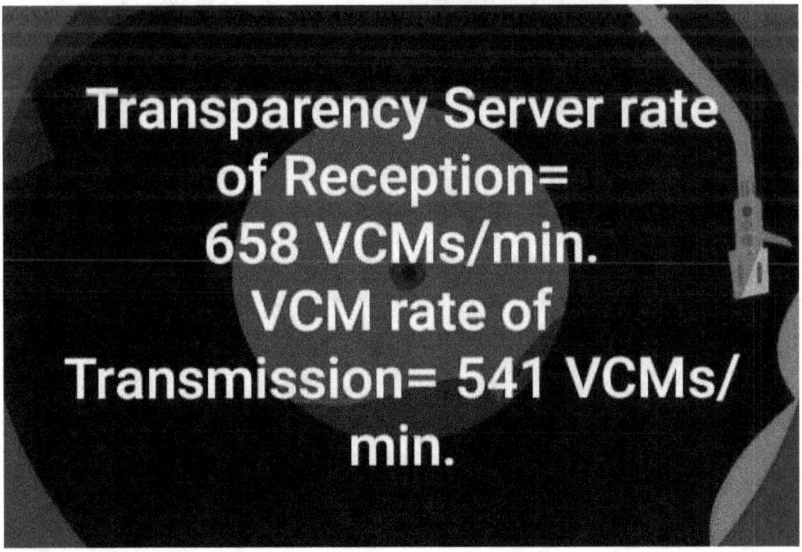

Transparency Server rate of Reception= 658 VCMs/min.
VCM rate of Transmission= 541 VCMs/min.

RECEPTION logs peaked at the 1st HOUR. TRANSMISSION logs peaked at the 2nd HOUR. May nag–MATCH ba sa mga datos?

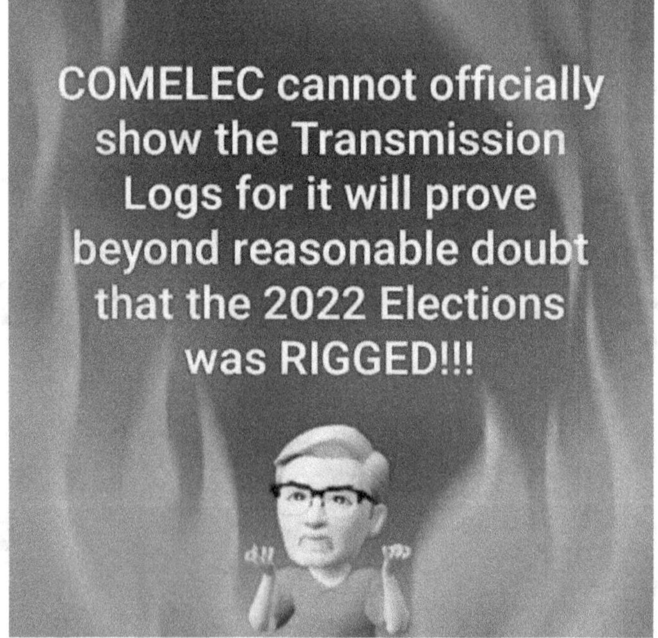
COMELEC cannot officially show the Transmission Logs for it will prove beyond reasonable doubt that the 2022 Elections was RIGGED!!!

ooooooo

Franklin Ysaac +